The Demons of Barack H. Obama

How the Gift of Discerning of Spirits
Reveals Unseen Forces
Influencing American Politics

Gordon James Klingenschmitt, PhD

© 2012, Gordon James Klingenschmitt, PhD

http://ObamasDemons.com

The Demons of Barack H. Obama is a non-fiction book explaining a practical, Biblical, Christian theology concerning the spiritual gift of discerning of spirits, which is generally described in the Bible as the supernatural ability God gives to some people to see otherwise invisible non-human spirits including the Holy Spirit of God, angels, and demons.

Because these invisible spirits influence human moral activity, and whisper suggestions to our human free will in the form of consolation (grace) and desolation (temptation), they try to gain access to our willful consent, so they can manifest in our human character, as explained by Ignatius of Loyola, the 16th century saint who founded the Society of Jesus (Jesuits) and wrote the *Rules for the Discerning of Spirits.*

By understanding the Biblical and Ignatian teaching about how to discern the agenda and activity of angels, demons, and the Holy Spirit as they interact with our human morality, we can begin to examine specific moral decisions made by individual human actors, to discern whether those humans consented to allow manifestations of the Holy Spirit or the devil in their free will cooperative choices.

By objectively observing the moral fruit, character, and manifestations of human actors, we can see how God (or the devil) uses people to build their moral (or immoral) kingdoms in our midst, particularly in the field of American politics. By associating spiritual discernment with human ethics, we can see with our spiritual eyes the otherwise invisible Spirit of God manifesting in politicians whose policies and laws promote moral holiness, truth, and love for God and neighbor, to build a godly nation.

However, by objectively observing how a politician's policies and laws may ultimately promote sin and immorality among the people, we can discern that politician actually manifesting demons, to destroy a nation.

This book examines the policies and actions of Barack H. Obama, to compare the moral indicators of his political behavior to Biblical standards of ethical morality, to help us discern what spirits are actually manifesting inside the soul of the 44th President of the United States.

Gordon James Klingenschmitt earned his PhD in Theology by writing his dissertation on the Gift of Discerning of Spirits and Church Ethics, in dialog with Ignatius of Loyola and other Biblical theologians. He is also the former Navy Chaplain who took a stand for the right to pray publicly "in Jesus' name" which cost him a 16-year military career, but he was later vindicated by Congress, who restored free speech rights for other chaplains. Please join his email list at prayinjesusname.org.

Join the discussion at: ObamasDemons.com

Cover Image by AP licensed for use.

http://ObamasDemons.com

GET TEN FREE COPIES OF THIS E-BOOK, NOW.

This e-book is available on AMAZON.COM for $2.95 U.S. and other outlets including CreateSpace.com and ObamasDemons.com.

This e-book & PDF are copyrighted, and may not be emailed.

However, if you purchased this e-book and email to us your e-receipt, you may obtain a FREE license to distribute the entire PDF of this e-book (as is), to up to 10 friends by email, so this e-book will be FREE for your 10 friends. Register now and email your receipt to license@obamasdemons.com. We will automatically email you a free distributor's license.

(FYI, the paperback for $9.95 is not part of this offer.)

GOT A LARGER EMAIL LIST?

You may also purchase a larger license to email this e-book more widely, to more than ten friends, at these rates:

License to email this e-book to:	Cost:
20 extra friends at 50 cents each	$ 9.95
50 extra friends at 40 cents each	$ 19.95
100 extra friends at 30 cents each	$ 29.95
200 friends at 20 cents each	$ 39.95
300 friends at 17 cents each	$ 49.95
500 friends at 14 cents each	$ 69.95
1000 friends at 10 cents each	$ 99.95

Over 1000 friends: $ 99.95 plus .05 per friend over 1000.

VISIT http://ObamasDemons.com TO BUY A LICENSE.

http://ObamasDemons.com

TABLE OF CONTENTS:

Introduction by the Author (GJK) ………………….. 5

Chapter 1: The Spiritual Gift of Discerning of Spirits….. 17

Chapter 2: Rules for Discerning of Spirits and Ignatian Pneumato-Ethical Method…………………….. 47

Chapter 3: Barack H. Obama's Demons Revealed (Events 1-25) …………………………………… 83

Chapter 4: More of Mr. Obama's Demons Revealed (Events 26-50) …………………………………… 143

Conclusion: The Demons Ruling Barack H. Obama….. 203

Is He the Anti-Christ?
    Afterword by Pastor Ernie Sanders………………… 209

About the Author: Who is GJK? ………………...…… 213

Introduction by the Author (GJK):

Democrat Congresswoman Maxine Waters (D-CA) recently delivered a fiery speech to delegates at the California Democratic State Convention, in which she referred to Republican House Speaker John Boehner (R-OH) and Majority Leader Eric Cantor (R-VA) as "demons." Her speech illustrated some apparent confusion about whether demons are people, or merely non-human spirits that influence people, and whether it is wise or even possible to "demonize" opposing candidates for political office. "I saw pictures of Boehner and Cantor on our screens," Waters said. "Don't ever let me see again in life those Republicans in our hall, on our screens, talking about anything. These are demons."[1] Her claim brought cheers from the crowd, but the political art of "demonizing" your opponents has become much more than political theatre. The political tactic is now commonplace, because it works, and helps win elections. It motivates crowds and resonates with voters for deep-seated, subconscious, and highly spiritual reasons.

---

[1] Maxine Waters (D-CA), Speech to California Democratic State Convention, (San Diego: 12 Feb 2012), http://www.youtube.com/watch?v=fpfwhWrvQZk Last viewed 16 Feb 12.

Having written and successfully defended my PhD theology dissertation on the biblical and spiritual gift of "discerning of spirits," examining the pneumatology[2] and church ethics of 16th century Saint Ignatius of Loyola, who wrote the *Rules for the Discerning of Spirits*,[3] I must admit the speech by Waters immediately caught my attention. Does the Democrat Congresswoman from California claim to have the supernatural gift from God, which gives her the ability to see otherwise invisible non-human spirits, including the Holy Spirit, angels, and demons? The holy gift and supernatural ability to see invisible spirits has been written about in the Bible, and throughout church history, but usually in a context reserved for saints and very holy people. As a former Navy Chaplain and ordained Pentecostal minister, I do not take the subject lightly, knowing from experience that God rarely graces even the holiest among us to accurately discern the spirits. I myself do not claim to always possess this gift, except in those rare occasions when I've been privileged to minister exorcism among the homeless or addicts to sin of many kinds, usually in the privacy of a confessional room.

---

[2] From the Greek word pneuma-, or spirit, and –tology, the study of spirits.
[3] Ignatius of Loyola, *The Spiritual Exercises of St. Ignatius: Based on Studies in the Language of the Autograph*, trans. Louis J. Puhl (Chicago: Loyola University Press, 1951), 141-150.

More recently, and because of my own experience having taken a stand to defend the free speech rights of military chaplains who pray publicly "in Jesus' name" in uniform, (which cost my career but earned my later vindication by the U.S. Congress), I have become interested in how spiritual forces influence American politics. I have traveled America, preached in 100+ churches in 27 states, and led mass petition drives that organized and delivered over four million fax petitions to legislatures, restoring the right to pray publicly "in Jesus' name" in 10 states. Since my honorable discharge I have worked in politics full time for four years, analyzing and writing about the spiritual battle for the political soul of America, which (combined with my Bachelor's degree in Political Science from the Air Force Academy) has led me to ask, how do politics and spirituality intersect? Can non-human spirits be discerned as they influence American politicians? Can any academic theologian, if truly gifted by God to see the Holy Spirit, angels, and demons, discern what influence those hidden spirits have upon American politics today, working in, for example, the person seated in our nation's highest office? This possibility has led me to prayerfully try to discern the spiritual forces of good and evil, which influence the 44th

President of the United States, a man for whom I pray regularly, Barack H. Obama.

WHAT THIS BOOK IS NOT:

This book is not my attempt to "demonize" President Barack H. Obama, or make him into one of many anti-Christs (despite Pastor Sanders' afterward), which is not even theoretically possible, since only Mr. Obama can do that, by his own willful consent to agree or disagree with the Holy Spirit or demonic forces. My words or observations cannot cause demons to enter Mr. Obama, nor could any of my own critics theoretically cause demons to enter my own soul, which inhabitation may only be granted by each of our own moral consent to choose our own sins. All political opponents can really do to each other is attempt, through prayerful and professional academic dialogue, to observe, discuss, and reveal the sins and spirits already present in the observed person's soul before we arrived. We can at best expose the demons already there, but we are not the cause of them.

This book is not an attempt to suggest that Mr. Obama is not personally a Christian. Since he claims that he is, we can trust that Mr. Obama's personal confession of Christ by his own words reveals the likely presence of Christ in some part of his soul, since "no one can say, 'Jesus is Lord,' except by the Holy Spirit." (1 Cor. 12:3, NASB). The presence of the Holy Spirit may be properly discerned in every holy human act or deed, including those of Mr. Obama. Yet even his confession does not guarantee his eternal salvation, since many who say to Jesus, "Lord, Lord," will hear him reply, "Depart from me, I never knew you."[4] I see some evidence, but I do not know for certain, if Mr. Obama is saved or lost. I'm not his judge; I'm only a humble messenger, speaking whatever truth I'm commissioned to carry.

This book is not an attempt to blame anybody's sins on the devil. The devil did not make Mr. Obama do anything. Contrary to the blame-shifting theology of the murderous Son of Sam who claimed "the devil made me do it," the Bible places 100% of human responsibility for sin upon our own human shoulders, mine included.

This book is not a prideful attempt to exalt my own morality over Mr. Obama's morality. I am not claiming to be more holy or godly than he. On the contrary, I am among the worst of sinners,[5] redeemed and forgiven by grace through faith in Jesus Christ, as Mr. Obama is possibly also. We who

---

[4] See Matt. 7:21-23.
[5] See Luke 18:13.

have studied and know the scriptures will be held more accountable than those who do not.[6] Trust me when I say that I hate my own sins and demons more than anyone else's. But I try to love God supremely, and neighbor equal to self, for this is the path to eternal life.[7]

This book does not endorse or oppose Mr. Obama for re-election. Churches may therefore legally distribute this book as religious education material. This book is not an attempt to say that Republicans are holier than Democrats, or vice-versa, or that any one group of people has more demons than any other. I do not claim any one sin is worse than any other, since every human sin is equally demonic.

Nor is any sin unforgivable except that of rejecting the forgiveness offered by Jesus when he died for our sins on the cross, or blaspheming the Holy Spirit.[8] For example, homosexuality and abortion are more loudly debated in political discourse, not because those private or individual human sins are worse than adultery and murder (they are not worse), rather because those sins are endorsed as praiseworthy and even subsidized with monetary benefits by some official government policies, while adultery and murder

---

[6] See James 3:1.
[7] See Luke 10:25-28.
[8] See Matt. 12:31-32.

are not. Some government policies promote demonic activity in people, and actually reward them for their sins. Government must never do that. It has no right, since rights ultimately come from God, who opposes all sin.

This book is not an attempt to see a demon behind every tree, or behind every human choice. Most choices do not involve any morality; for example there is no demonic or angelic influence behind our daily choice of soup, salad, or sandwich for lunch. God gives great liberty to mankind, to choose among many options not forbidden, and therefore not demonic. However, in the field of moral choices, when we knowingly and willfully choose that which God forbids, we certainly invite demonic involvement. The devil will eagerly rush in to rule our hearts whenever we sin, because we willfully invite him to rule our immorality. "Do not sin…do not give the devil a foothold," (Eph. 4:26-27, NIV).

This book is not a call for any action, except prayer, by any reader toward Mr. Obama. Before I get falsely accused,
I hereby denounce anyone with racist motives or violent tendencies. As the chaplain of the 2008 national campaign to elect Alan Keyes as President, I honor the words of Dr. Martin Luther King who prayed we could "live in a nation

where [people] will not be judged by the color of their skin but by the content of their character."[9] This book examines Mr. Obama's character.

Finally, this book is not an attempt to say that Mr. Obama is demon *possessed*. I avoid the word possessed, which has been hijacked by false Hollywood imagery. It is more accurate to say that when he promotes morally good policies that promote true and biblical holiness among mankind, Mr. Obama is *ruled* by the Holy Spirit, but when he promotes evil policies that promote sin among mankind, Mr. Obama is *ruled* by demons, which evil spirits we can discern by the moral fruit they produce, in the man and in other humans who follow his ideas. Jesus instructed us how to discern the spirits: "Beware of the false prophets…you will know them by their fruits," (Matt 7:15-16, NASB).

WHAT THIS BOOK IS:

This book is a professional, academic application of Ignatius of Loyola's *Rules for Discerning of Spirits* to American politics, using a specific theological method, which I created and successfully defended to earn my PhD, the Ignatian Pneumato-Ethical Method (IPEM) also known as the

---

[9] Dr. Martin Luther King, "I have a dream" (Washington, D.C. 28 Aug 1963).

Discerning of Spirits Theological Method (DSTM). This method requires understanding the necessary theological connection between non-human spirits and human morals. The thesis of my PhD dissertation,[10] which I will not attempt to defend again here, was that "the spiritual gift of discerning of spirits, especially as that gift is understood by Ignatius of Loyola, is foundational to ecclesial ethics, because spiritual discernment supports ethical formation and judgment and, conversely, ethics is foundational to spiritual discernment." Or in simple terms, ethics and spirits are interdependent. We cannot morally discern right from wrong unless we first discern the Holy Spirit from the devil, and conversely, we cannot discern the Holy Spirit from the devil unless we morally discern right from wrong.

    Because we can objectively examine the moral fruit of a person's words and deeds, and because ethics and spirits are interdependent, we can discern or see a reflection of the otherwise invisible non-human spirits that rule human hearts. Our inner demons are revealed by our outer vices, and our inner Holy Spirit is revealed by our outer virtues. As the

---

[10] Gordon James Klingenschmitt, "Discerning the Spirits in Ecclesial Ethics: Ignatius of Loyola and the Pneumatological Foundations of Ecclesiology," PhD. diss. (Virginia Beach: Regent University, 2012). Available in most academic libraries through the global dissertation database.

Apostle Paul explained, love, joy, peace, patience, kindness, goodness, gentleness, faithfulness and self-control reveal the person of the Holy Spirit manifesting from within our soul.[11] As Jesus explained, "The good man out of the good treasure of his heart brings forth what is good; and the evil man out of the evil treasure brings forth what is evil; for his mouth speaks from that which fills his heart," (Luke 6:45, NASB). If a person is filled with the Holy Spirit of God, their words and deeds will display moral holiness, which is a manifestation of the Holy Spirit. If a person is filled with and ruled by demons, their words and deeds will manifest outward sin, which is a manifestation of the demonic. By observing a person's sin, we can clearly and objectively discern their otherwise invisible demons.

    This book is therefore a revelatory examination of the non-human spirits that influence our national policies, and express themselves through our national political ethics. This book is a spiritual, biblical, pneumatological analysis of the objective moral indicators found in speeches and actions of the executive who occupies the White House, which can help reveal to us the spirits operating around and inside his soul.

---

[11] See Galatians 5:22-23.

This book is an explanation of the kingdom of God and the kingdom of the devil as those two kingdoms battle and manifest in American politics, particularly in the locus of the mind, heart, and soul of one man, President Barack H. Obama.

In the first two chapters, I will explain the spiritual gift of "discerning of spirits," as it is described in the Bible and in the Ignatian *Rules*, to provide a background for application of the Ignatian Pneumato-Ethical Method to analyze Mr. Obama's practices and policies. In the next two chapters, I will examine 50 historic events that reveal Mr. Obama's policies, comparing their moral fruit and political outcomes to biblical standards of right and wrong, to try to discern whether he was personally influenced by, or ruled by, the Holy Spirit or demons while promoting his moral or immoral policies. In the fifth and final chapter, I will conclude by exposing and revealing…

    The Demons of Barack H. Obama.

GET TEN FREE COPIES OF THIS E-BOOK, NOW.

This e-book is available on AMAZON.COM for $2.95 U.S. and other outlets including CreateSpace.com and ObamasDemons.com. This e-book & PDF are copyrighted, and may not be emailed. However, if you purchased this e-book and email to us your e-receipt, you may obtain a FREE license to distribute the entire PDF of this e-book (as is), to up to 10 friends by email, so this e-book will be FREE for your 10 friends. Register now and email your receipt to license@obamasdemons.com. We will automatically email you a free distributor's license. (FYI, the paperback for $9.95 is not part of this offer.)

GOT A LARGER EMAIL LIST?

You may also purchase a larger license to email this e-book more widely, to more than ten friends, at these rates:

License to email this e-book to:	Cost:
20 extra friends at 50 cents each	$ 9.95
50 extra friends at 40 cents each	$ 19.95
100 extra friends at 30 cents each	$ 29.95
200 friends at 20 cents each	$ 39.95
300 friends at 17 cents each	$ 49.95
500 friends at 14 cents each	$ 69.95
1000 friends at 10 cents each	$ 99.95
Over 1000 friends:	$ 99.95 plus .05 per friend over 1000.

VISIT http://ObamasDemons.com TO BUY A LICENSE.

CHAPTER 1: The Spiritual Gift of Discerning of Spirits

Before we can try to discern the demons of Barack H. Obama, we must first understand the spiritual gift of discerning of spirits. The Bible describes nine spiritual gifts among the charismata of the Holy Spirit of God, listed by the Apostle Paul:

"There are varieties of gifts, but the same Spirit. And there are varieties of ministries, and the same Lord. There are varieties of effects, but the same God who works all things in all persons. But to each one is given the manifestation of the Spirit for the common good. For to one is given the **word of wisdom** through the Spirit, and to another the **word of knowledge** according to the same Spirit; to another **faith** by the same Spirit, and to another **gifts of healing** by the one Spirit, and to another the **effecting of miracles**, and to another **prophecy**, and to another the **distinguishing of spirits**, to another various kinds of **tongues**, and to another the **interpretation of tongues**. But one and the same Spirit works all these things, distributing to each one individually just as He wills," (1 Cor. 12:4-11, NASB, emphasis added).

The distinguishing or "discerning of spirits" (transliterated Greek: *diakrisis pneumaton*), is clearly described here as a supernatural gift from God, given to some followers of Christ, enabling them to see and distinguish otherwise invisible spirits. We do not control the gift, which is given to some as the Holy Spirit wills. Not everybody has this special, supernatural gift from God, nor does any one person have it all the time, including me. In fact most people cannot see angels, demons, or the Holy Spirit, at all, since they are invisible to humans without a supernatural revelation from God, Who must graciously open our spiritual eyes to see them. But when you truly receive the gift, you can often see the spirits, plain as day. Those who have seen spirits understand what I mean. Those who have not, likely do not.

WHAT ARE THE FOUR KINDS OF SPIRITS?

There are four kinds of spirits described in the Bible: God, angels, demons, and humans. Humans live in the natural, physical realm with physical bodies and physical eyes that allow us to see natural, physical objects. God, angels, and demons, however, live in a spiritual realm without physical bodies. We cannot see them with our natural eyes, rather we can only see them if we are gifted by

God to use our spiritual eyes. Without the gift of spiritual eyesight, humans remain spiritually blind, which explains why many atheists deny the existence of God, angels, and demons, whom they cannot see.

God is always invisible to our physical eyes, but God is not invisible to our spiritual eyes, if we humbly prepare ourselves to receive the gift of discerning of spirits. The gift enables us to see what atheists cannot, which helps us believe in what we really see with the eyes of our faith, while they remain blind and limited by their lack of experience. This explains why Jesus encouraged us to pray that God would "open their eyes so that they may turn from darkness to light and from the dominion of Satan to God, that they may receive forgiveness of sins and an inheritance among those who have been sanctified by faith in Me," (Acts 26:18, NASB). If you are not yet a believer, that's OK, I sympathize, and I was once in your shoes. I merely want to help you see what I've now seen, so please pray, simply and humbly, that God will open your eyes to see Him, and soon you will discern His Spirit.

Humans are spirits, created in the image of God. Let's all say this out loud: "I am an eternal spirit (my heart, the core of my identity), I have a soul (mind, will and emotions), and I live in a temporary physical body."[12] Your spirit or heart is your core identity, eternal and created in the image of the Spirit of God, which can be ruled by God, and is intended to reflect the moral character of God with love, joy, peace, patience, kindness, goodness, faithfulness, gentleness, and self-control.[13] That eternal moral character (love) is who God made you to be, and your spirit will live on forever, even after your body dies, in either heaven or hell.

The Bible teaches that human spirits are judged immediately upon death; we do not reincarnate and we cannot walk the earth as ghosts after we die, contrary to popular myth or false religion. Haunted houses and ghost tours are popular, but if you really see a ghost, it is more likely a demon impersonating a human, since it is not a human spirit. The Bible is clear: "It is appointed for men to die once and after this comes judgment," (Heb. 9:27, NASB). Jesus taught human spirits, after the death of their physical bodies, can never return from heaven or hell to earth.[14] You will never meet the ghost of a dead human on earth, but demons imitating humans are common, and should be discerned.

---

[12] See 1 Thess. 4:23.
[13] See Gal. 5:22-23.
[14] See Luke 16:26.

Your soul is composed of your mind (thoughts), free will (choices), and emotions (feelings). Your body is confined to this physical world, which you experience with five senses of sight, hearing, touch, taste, and smell. Our bodily senses are natural, but our spiritual senses are supernatural, and we can "because of practice have [our] senses trained to discern good and evil," (Heb. 5:14, NASB). We sense physical things with our five senses, but we sense spiritual things by discerning their morality, not their physicality.

Moral discernment of right and wrong is the first step toward spiritual discernment of the Holy Spirit from the devil. Right and wrong cannot be touched with our hands, but we know right and wrong in our hearts, because we see morality with the spiritual eyes of our hearts. Practice holiness, and soon you will "see" the otherwise invisible Holy Spirit with your moral senses, because He rules your heart, and so he will become obvious to your internal spiritual sense of right and wrong. God is Holy. When we see holiness, we see God. But if you cannot discern holiness from sin, neither can you discern God from the devil.

God is a Spirit. He does not need a physical body, except He chose to inhabit one when God became man, and incarnated himself in the person of Jesus, to experience life in our shoes. Manifest to us as the Son of God, Jesus taught us that "God is spirit, and those who worship Him must worship in spirit and truth," (John 4:24, NASB). Jesus had the gift of discerning of spirits, the supernatural ability to see the Holy Spirit of God, in the person of God the Father, in the person of the Holy Spirit, and in Himself, ruling his own heart and morality.

The Holy Spirit was invisible to others around Jesus without the gift of discerning of spirits, for example to Nicodemus, whom Jesus rebuked because he could not see the Holy Spirit as wind among trees, but claimed to be Israel's teacher.[15] (If you can't discern spirits, don't try to teach others about spiritual matters.)

John the Baptist was supernaturally gifted to see the Holy Spirit descending upon Jesus as a dove at his water baptism, whom apparently nobody else saw.[16] Jesus was able to discern the secret thoughts, hearts, and spirits of men,[17] and in the same breath Jesus said he saw both the Holy Spirit and Satan ruling the heart of Peter.[18] Why could Jesus see

---

[15] See John 3:3-13.
[16] See Matt. 3:16.
[17] See John 2:25.
[18] See Matt. 16:17-23.

the Holy Spirit and Satan both ruling Peter's heart in nearly the same moment, when nobody else could discern those spirits in Peter? Jesus had the supernatural gift, as given to him by the Holy Spirit, Who ruled Jesus' heart with moral perfection.

Later, after Peter received that same Baptism in the Holy Spirit, he was supernaturally gifted to see the devil inside the hearts of Ananias and Sapphira, when nobody else could. "Ananias, why has Satan filled your heart to lie to the Holy Spirit?" Peter asked (Acts 5:3, NASB), and accurately discerned the evil spirits ruling the hearts of two liars, before they fell over dead, and God proved Peter was right.

Angels are spirits, described in the Bible as invisible messengers,[19] comforters,[20] worshippers,[21] and warriors[22] who help God and morally agree with God. On rare occasion they are revealed to humans, appearing for example to Mary at her immaculate conception,[23] to the shepherds in the fields announcing Jesus' birth,[24] to Elijah who prayed God would

---

[19] See for example, the Archangel Gabriel in Daniel 8-9 and Luke 1:11-20, 26-38.
[20] See Matt 4:11.
[21] See Rev. 4, 5.
[22] See for example, the Archangel Michael in Daniel 10, 12; Jude 1:9 and Rev. 12:7.
[23] See Luke 1:28.
[24] See Luke 2:8-14.

open the eyes of Elisha who saw armies of angels,[25] and to countless other saints in the Bible and throughout church history. Angels do not however, as far as the Bible describes, try to inhabit the hearts of humans, as demons or the Holy Spirit do.

Demons are spirits, described in the Bible as the enemies of God, invisible spiritual beings who morally disagree with God and who tempt humans to sin, and invade the hearts of people to dwell in us and rule our human hearts with evil. Perhaps one-third of all the angels who rebelled against God followed the angel Lucifer (who became the demon Satan) when he fell from heaven.[26] Satan is the chief demon, but he is not omnipresent, everywhere simultaneously, as the Spirit of God is. Satan is one finite being in one location, but he rules over innumerable demons who act as his personal agents, and carry out his agenda everywhere, especially wherever human sin and temptation can be found. When the Bible therefore talks about many different people "possessed of the devil" it does not mean they are all filled simultaneously with the person of Satan

---

[25] "Then Elisha prayed and said, "O LORD, I pray, open his eyes that he may see." And the LORD opened the servant's eyes and he saw; and behold, the mountain was full of horses and chariots of fire all around Elisha." 2 Kings 6:17, NASB.
[26] See Isaiah 14:12-14 and Luke 10:17-20.

himself, rather they are filled with demons who represent Satan vicariously. This explains why, when some talk generically of the devil, they actually mean many devils or demons, not specifically the finite person of Satan himself, whose name I would mention if I meant his singular person.

Demons or devils do not have physical bodies of their own. Having lost their battle with God in heaven; they were condemned to wander the earth in torment. Jesus describes their painful condition, full of craving and jealousy without a bodily outlet to express their evil rebellion, so demons seek peace by inhabiting us humans, borrowing our bodies to express their evil personality, as a puppet-master who animates a puppet. For example Jesus said, "Now when the unclean spirit goes out of a man, it **passes through waterless places seeking rest, and does not find it.** Then it says, 'I will return to my house from which I came'; and when it comes, it finds it unoccupied, swept, and put in order. Then it goes and takes along with it seven other spirits more wicked than itself, and they go in and live there; and the last state of that man becomes worse than the first," (Matt. 12:43-45, NASB, emphasis added).

My friend Pastor Henry Wright used to say, "When the devil is inside us, he is at peace and we are in torment.

But when we kick the devil out of us, we are at peace and he is in torment."[27] Demons crave human flesh. Demons wander in terrible pain if we do not sin, which is why they tempt us to sin, so they can gain permission to move into our bodies, so they can find peace. Not only do we know *why*, we also know *how* they gain access to indwell us: by tempting us to sin. Human sin opens the door to demonic invasion.

THE CONNECTION BETWEEN DEMONS AND SIN:

There exists an interdependent connection between demons and human sin. For example, the Bible describes the fall of man from sinless, perfect obedience to God, into a state of sinful, rebellious disobedience to God, well documented in Genesis 3 when Adam and Eve were tempted by Satan to sin. In Satan's first appearance in the Bible, we see his agenda to tempt humans to sin, and he hasn't changed that agenda. Devils do this by lying to us about God's commands. If a demon can get us to disobey God's commands, he can gain entry. Yet by our obedience to God, the Holy Spirit rules us.

---

[27] Pastor Henry Wright, Pleasant Valley Church, Thomaston, Georgia, http://pleasantvalleychurch.net

For example, we can discern Satan's plan to indwell Eve's morality, by her own moral transformation from resister of temptation to temptress. Eve's moral character changed dramatically, revealing that she actually took into herself the moral character of Satan. First the devil was inside the snake tempting the woman, then the devil was inside the woman tempting the man, then the devil was inside the man lying to and hiding from God. The devil invaded and moved into their hearts and bodies through their voluntary consent to sin.

But temptation is not the same as sin. Temptation is when the evil spirit is outside of us whispering to gain our moral consent; sin is when we consent to allow the evil spirit to rule inside of our heart and display its evil moral character through our personality. Jesus was tempted by Satan, but Jesus did not sin, so he was never ruled by Satan.[28] But we, like puppets, do what the master inside of us commands for us to do. Satan rules our moral hearts every time we disobey God. But the good news is, God rules our moral hearts every time we obey God. There are no exceptions to this rule. "Do you not know that when you present yourselves to someone as slaves for obedience, you are slaves of the one whom you

---

[28] See Matt. 4:1-11.

obey, either of sin resulting in death, or of obedience resulting in righteousness?" (Romans 6:16, NASB). Morally, we are either slaves to God or the devil. There is no middle option. When God commands us to love our neighbor, we may either obey or disobey, but there is no "neutrality" in true love.

The Second Century Christian writer Shepherd of Hermas described the spiritual war between the opposing non-human spirits who simultaneously inhabit human hearts: "Be patient…for **if you be patient, the Holy Spirit that dwells in you will be pure**. He will not be darkened by any evil spirit, but…he will rejoice and be glad…having great peace within himself. But if any outburst of anger take place, immediately the Holy Spirit, who is tender, is straitened, not having a pure place, and He seeks to depart. For he is choked by the vile spirit, and cannot attend on the Lord as he wishes, for anger pollutes him. For the Lord dwells in long-suffering, but the devil in anger. **The two spirits, then, when dwelling in the same habitation, are at discord with each other**, and are troublesome to that man in whom they dwell."[29]

---

[29] The Pastor of Hermas, "Book II, Commandment 5:1," *The Ante-Nicene Fathers: Translations of The Writings of the Fathers down to A.D. 325.*, vol. II., ed. Alexander Roberts, James Donaldson and A. Cleveland Coxe. (Buffalo: The

That's worth reading again and again. "The two spirits, then, when dwelling in the same habitation, are at discord with each other, and are troublesome to the man in whom they dwell."

CAN A CHRISTIAN HAVE A DEMON?

Can two spirits, the Holy Spirit and the devil, simultaneously rule the heart of a Christian? Yes and no. Second century writer Shepherd of Hermas clearly said yes, but I wish to qualify his answer. Patience is an attribute of the Holy Spirit, but He cannot rule that part of our character at the same time a demon of Impatience rules us. Either you're patient or you're impatient. It's a binary option, only one or the other is logically possible in a particular moment. So no, the Holy Spirit and a demon cannot simultaneously rule the "patience" part of your moral character.

Yet patience and kindness are two distinct facets of the same Holy Spirit. Is it possible for a human to be patient, and unkind, simultaneously? Yes, because our human character is morally multi-faceted, made in the image of God, with free

---

Christian Literature Publishing Co., 1885-87; Peabody, Mass.: Hendrickson, 1994), 23, emphasis added.

will concerning every moral facet, independently. We can be cruel and patient simultaneously, but we cannot be cruel and kind simultaneously. It is therefore possible for one part of our moral character to be ruled by the Holy Spirit of patience, while an entirely different part of our moral character is ruled by a demon of cruelty. **"The two spirits, then, when dwelling in the same habitation, are at discord with each other,** and are troublesome to that man in whom they dwell."

There are thousands of virtues and vices possible. It is therefore possible, and actually quite common, for Christians to be morally mature in many aspects of their character which are ruled by God, and immorally immature in many other facets of their character which are still ruled by sin and the devil. This reality requires our minds be sanctified and renewed by God's Word to transform every part of our moral character,[30] until we grow up into the perfect image of Christ.[31] Therefore I conclude the Holy Spirit and demons can rule different moral parts of the same person, but not the same moral part of the same person. Our job as "Spirit-filled" Christians is to evict the wrong spirits, and welcome the Holy Spirit until we are entirely sanctified, so the Holy

---

[30] See Rom. 12:1-2.
[31] See Eph. 4:12-13.

Spirit rules every moral part of our heart, mind, soul, and strength. When every part of your moral character is truly ruled by Christ, then He is certainly able to keep you safe from demons, and you have nothing to fear. As Evangelist Reinhard Bonnke says, "Flies don't land on a hot stove," meaning if you live a life of true holiness, demons will not rule you, because sin does not rule you.

Am I saying that Christians can be demon "possessed," or merely "oppressed?" We must answer the question Biblically, or not at all. I make no distinction between these two words, because the Bible uses them identically. Only one scripture, Acts 10:38 talks of those "oppressed by the devil," but it uses the same context as 14 other scriptures in Matthew, Mark, Luke, and Acts that describe those "possessed with devils." Some suggest "oppression" means the evil spirit is outside us tempting us, and "possession" implies the demon is inside us sinning through us. This is mostly true, but since I avoid these words, I will make a better distinction, asking simply whether we are "ruled" by sin and demons, or "ruled" by holy love and the Holy Spirit. Is Jesus Christ the Lord of your heart? If yes, then you must also be ruled by love for God and neighbor.

If you only claim with your lips that Jesus is your Lord, but in reality your morals are ruled by sin, then you are ruled by devils, even if you claim to be a Christian. Most Christians think they could not possibly be demon possessed, because that's only something they see in Hollywood movies. "Oh, I can sin quite a bit, and not invite the devil to rule my heart," argue the naïve and corrupt. But the Bible clearly says otherwise. "You are slaves to the one whom you obey—whether you are slaves to sin, which leads to death, or to obedience, which leads to righteousness," (Rom. 6:16, NIV).

Do you really think you can be a slave to sin, and not a slave to demons? "The one who practices sin is of the devil; for the devil has sinned from the beginning...By this the children of God and the children of the devil are obvious: anyone who does not practice righteousness is not of God," (1 John 3:8, 10, NASB). This scripture makes it clear. If you sin, then that part of you is ruled by the devil, period.

What is exorcism? If every human sin always invites the devil to rule our hearts, then every act of true repentance is simultaneously an act of exorcism, evicting the devil or his demons from our hearts. Every act of holiness invites the

Holy Spirit to baptize us with the fire of His love, with His true moral fruit, and with His spiritual gifts.

People think of exorcism as some rare and dramatic event that requires a priest holding a crucifix and splashing holy water, like they've seen in some B-rated vampire movie. I do not. As a minister who has cast demons out of scores of people, I can tell you that exorcism is as simple and common as truly repenting of your sins. You can evict the devil from yourself, without a priest, because Jesus is our High Priest and He is present to help you escape the addiction of sin, if you will simply renounce all your known sins and demons, and sincerely invite the Spirit of Christ to rule your heart with true holiness. He will do this now, today, immediately, if You invite Him to rule your heart.

Often when I truly repent of a known sin, I feel a shudder or a chill as the evil spirit departs, and sudden joy and often tears as the Holy Spirit enters that part of my renewed character. I am constantly self-evaluating and confessing my sins to God, daily inviting His Spirit Baptism, which keeps my heart full of love toward God and neighbor. We should all practice daily repentance, which can keep the parasites from inhabiting our souls, and welcome the King of Kings to rule and indwell us as His holy temple.

SIN IS NOT HUMAN UNTIL WE CONSENT

Anger is a non-human spirit. Lust is a non-human spirit. After we consent, these non-human spirits begin to control us, and manifest inside our humanity. Shepherd of Hermas' image of two spirits dwelling in the same habitation, fighting at discord, and troublesome to the man in whom they dwell, evokes similar connotations to Paul's struggle between flesh and spirit in Romans 7:

"I am not practicing what I would like to do, but I am doing the very thing I hate. But if I do the very thing I do not want to do, I agree with the Law, confessing that the Law is good. So now, **no longer am I the one doing it,** but sin which dwells in me. For I know that nothing good dwells in me, that is, in my flesh; for the willing is present in me, but the doing of the good is not. For the good that I want, I do not do, but I practice the very evil that I do not want. But if I am doing the very thing I do not want, **I am no longer the one doing it,** but sin which dwells in me," (Romans 7:15-19, NASB, emphasis added).

Paul here describes sin as a non-human entity. Sin later becomes human because we consent to it by our free will (making us fully responsible), but sin is initially non-human because **we are not the ones doing it. Sin is doing**

us. Twice Paul repeats himself, saying "I am not the one doing it." Your sins are not an original part of your humanity, at least not the 'you' God originally created for you to become. Something outside of yourself, something non-human, is controlling you, inside of you, moving you according to its own agenda and its own will, and you feel powerless to stop.

So let's repeat aloud Paul's Biblical words: "I am not the one doing the sin." Something not human is doing the sin, inside of you. Every time you sin, you are ruled by an evil spirit, who manifests itself inside of you, and displays its evil personality through your members. It's not your spirit in control, and it's certainly not the Holy Spirit. It's an evil spirit to whom you have given control, by your voluntary free-will cooperation. Human sin is always, always a voluntary cooperation with the demonic.

The good news is, those evil spirits can be evicted, from you, and others around you. You have been delegated authority and redemption power! Jesus not only performed countless exorcisms in the Gospels, he also gave authority to his 12 disciples and all Christian believers since (including at least 70 anonymous disciples) to cast demons out of people.[32] Jesus had names for these evil spirits. He described them according to their moral conduct.

"The things that proceed out of the mouth come from the heart, and those defile the man. For out of the heart come **evil thoughts, murders, adulteries, fornications, thefts, false witness, slanders.** These are the things which defile the man" (Matt. 15:18-19, NASB, emphasis added).

Jesus named the demons: spirits of evil thoughts, spirits of murder, spirits of adultery and fornication, spirits of theft, lying, slander. Jesus discerned the non-human spirits according to the moral sins they manifest in human sins. Where do they dwell? Inside our hearts! Then they express their personalities through our words and deeds, which come out of our hearts.

The Bible calls this process a "manifestation." When the hidden demons are incarnate in our bodies and displayed through human flesh, they manifest (reveal) their hidden attributes by our immoral deeds. "Now the works of the flesh are **manifest**, which are these: Adultery, fornication, uncleanness…" (Gal. 5:19, NASB, emphasis added.) You

---

[32] See Matthew 10:1 and Luke 10:17-19.

can already begin to see the connection between the non-human spirits and our human morality.

HUMAN SIN IS ALWAYS, ALWAYS DEMONIC.

Some 'expert' theologians who think they're smarter than the Bible will argue that humans can sin repeatedly without giving the devil a foothold. What's that you argue? Sin is only our human flesh, and it's not demonic? Get behind me Satan. People who think that really must read their Bibles, and let it change our minds, so we can begin to discern the spirits who wish to remain hidden behind the lies we've learned from false teachers, who help the devil invade us. The Bible makes it crystal clear, that human sin is always, always demonic, with no exceptions:

"Little children, make sure no one deceives you; the one who practices righteousness is righteous, just as [Jesus] is righteous; **the one who practices sin is of the devil**; for the devil has sinned from the beginning. The Son of God appeared for this purpose, to destroy the works of the devil. No one who is born of God practices sin, because His seed abides in him; and he cannot sin, because he is born of God. By this the children of God and **the children of the devil are obvious: anyone who does not practice righteousness** is not of God, nor the one who does not love his brother," (1 John 3:6-10, NASB, emphasis added.)

Human sin is always, always demonic. To say otherwise, that you can sin freely without opening a door to allow the devil to rule your hearts, is at best naïve, and at worst a teaching promoted by the devil himself. "Oh don't worry, you can sin often, and I won't move into your heart," says the devil, and then he or his demons move into your heart and manifest their evil personality directly through your sin, every time you sin, and suddenly rule your house.

But the good news is, that true human holiness is always, always a manifestation of the Holy Spirit of God. Even the 'expert' theologians must admit Saint Augustine defeated the Pelagian heresy that we can be holy without prevenient grace and help from God.[33] Therefore we cannot be holy without simultaneously manifesting the Holy Spirit. Human holiness is never fully human. We don't initiate holiness; we only consent to the Spirit of Holiness who moves into us from outside of us. For example, we cannot possibly choose love, without God simultaneously moving

---

[33] "No one lives rightly without the grace of God." Augustine, "On the Proceedings of Pelagius," *The Fathers of the Church: A New Translation,* vol. 86 (Washington D.C.: Catholic University of America Press, 1992), 113.

into our heart and manifesting His own loving personality, manifest through our morality.

"No one has seen God [physically] at any time; [but] if we love one another, God abides in us, and His love is perfected in us," (1 John 4:12, NASB, brackets added).

The apostle is telling us how to see God, not physically but spiritually, by allowing love to rule our hearts. When we love, God moves into us, and we see Him revealed immediately, as the Holy Spirit manifests himself through our morality. "God is love, and the one who abides in love abides in God, and God abides in him," (1 John 4:16, NASB). Did you know, that every time you choose to love, God manifests His moral character in you, starting in your heart, then moving through your loving words and deeds? When you truly love God and neighbor, you can discern the Spirit of God, and you can "see" His invisible Spirit, because you experience God moving through your being, as love.

BIBLE EXPLAINS DISCERNING OF SPIRITS.

The clearest biblical explanation of the gift of discerning of spirits is in 1 John 4:1-6: "Beloved, do not believe every spirit, but **test the spirits to see whether they are from God,** because many false prophets have gone out into the world. By this you know the Spirit of God: every spirit that confesses that Jesus Christ has come in the flesh is from God; and every spirit that does not confess Jesus is not from God; this is the spirit of the Antichrist…greater is He who is in you than he who is in the world…We are from God; he who knows God listens to us; **he who is not from God does not listen to us. By this we know the spirit of truth and the spirit of error,**" (1 John 4:1-6, NASB, emphasis added). So wait, if we really know God, we'll always agree with the writers of the New Testament Bible?

Now we get to the bottom line. Here's how you can reliably discern the Holy Spirit from a demon. **People who are filled with the spirit of truth agree with the writers of the New Testament. People who are filled with demons of error disagree with the writers of the New Testament.** While that may seem shocking to the uninitiated, it provides a clear and immovable plumb line for success in all spiritual discernment. And here is why:

The disciples who walked with Jesus and wrote the gospels and epistles learned how to discern spirits, directly from The Master. You and I did not. Since the apostles learned how to properly discern spirits according to their manifestations, displayed in right and wrong morality, their ethical teachings have better, more reliable moral authority than yours, mine, or anyone else's, for the simple reason that they knew how to discern the spirits.

They saw the Holy Spirit and the devil more clearly than we do, therefore they perceived more accurately the moral graces of the Holy Spirit and immoral temptations of Satan, which gives their moral teachings better accuracy when defining right and wrong. If you disagree with the moral teachings of those who learned directly from the Spirit of Christ, then you disagree with the Holy Spirit Himself, and you are a false prophet. You will look at the Spirit of Christ, listen to his teachings, and say "no, that's a demon, we better not obey his moral teachings." You will commit the unforgivable sin of blaspheming the Holy Spirit, by calling Him a demon.[34] You may claim to properly discern the spirits, but if you fail to obey Jesus' teachings, you are deceived and a deceiver, not only manifesting sin and Satan in yourself, but also promoting evil in your followers.

After that sobering warning, please let me conclude this chapter with a more encouraging word from Jesus, about how we can all properly receive the gift to discern spirits with greater accuracy. This is especially directed to help those

---

[34] See Matt. 12:24.

"Christian" teachers who disagree with the Bible, and hold their own immoral opinions higher than the authority of the New Testament:

"You hypocrite, first take the log out of your own eye, and then you will see clearly to take the speck out of your brother's eye," (Matt. 7:5, NASB).

While this at first may seem confrontational, it's actually a helpful lesson from Jesus about how to receive the spiritual gift of discerning of spirits. The reason we cannot accurately discern the spirits in other peoples' hearts, is that our own hearts are unclean, and we ourselves are full of evil. Our own demons cause our own spiritual blindness.

People ask me, "Chaps, I've never seen the Holy Spirit, where is he hiding?" I answer that He hides behind our sins. If our sins were removed, the scales would fall from our spiritual eyes, and we would receive the gift to see Him clearly. I cannot count the number of times when I led people to see and discern the Holy Spirit, very personally and powerfully, simply by helping them renounce their sins, and inviting the Spirit of Christ to rule our hearts. When the Spirit of Christ rules your heart, you will see Him revealed as the exact same love you feel and manifest toward God and neighbor. But when your heart remains full of selfishness, you cannot logically experience love flowing through you, so you cannot see or experience that love, and you cannot see God flowing through you. You remain blind to the invisible God, simply because you have not invited Him to rule you.

But when He truly rules you, you will discern His Spirit ruling inside of you, as love. To see God, you must truly obey His command to love God and neighbor. When love rules your heart as Lord of your entire morality, you will see God. He must first be Lord, and only then will He be revealed in us.

There is a direct synergy between our own moral self-examination, and our ability to see. I must not look first for demons or evil spirits inside other people, not even Barack H. Obama, until I have first looked into my own heart. When you really begin to operate in the gift of discerning of spirits, the first place you will see them is in your own heart. When my heart is truly clean, only then will God enable me to see into others' hearts, so I can help them get clean too. It may take years of self-examination, prayer and fasting before we are empowered to see into others' hearts.

Perhaps you could pray with me, as I write the following prayer for myself too:

A HUMBLE PRAYER FOR DISCERNMENT:

"God I repent for my own sins first. God help me remove the log from my own eye first, right now, today. Then when my own heart is clean, please equip me to see more accurately into the hearts of others, not so I may judge them, but so I may help them know God. Let the church be holy first, before we attempt to clean up the political culture. Jesus, rule our hearts today, and fill us with your Holy Spirit, as we willfully consent to allow God's true moral character to indwell us, and manifest Your holiness through our words and deeds. We renounce all our known sins and demons. Get them out of us, so we can see clearly to minister the forgiveness of Christ to others, and begin to exorcise and cast out the demons in the world around us. In Jesus' name, Amen."

http://ObamasDemons.com

GET TEN FREE COPIES OF THIS E-BOOK, NOW.

This e-book is available on AMAZON.COM for $2.95 U.S. and other outlets including CreateSpace.com and ObamasDemons.com. This e-book & PDF are copyrighted, and may not be emailed. However, if you purchased this e-book and email to us your e-receipt, you may obtain a FREE license to distribute the entire PDF of this e-book (as is), to up to 10 friends by email, so this e-book will be FREE for your 10 friends. Register now and email your receipt to license@obamasdemons.com. We will automatically email you a free distributor's license. (FYI, the paperback for $9.95 is not part of this offer.)

GOT A LARGER EMAIL LIST?

You may also purchase a larger license to email this e-book more widely, to more than ten friends, at these rates:

License to email this e-book to:	Cost:
20 extra friends at 50 cents each	$ 9.95
50 extra friends at 40 cents each	$ 19.95
100 extra friends at 30 cents each	$ 29.95
200 friends at 20 cents each	$ 39.95
300 friends at 17 cents each	$ 49.95
500 friends at 14 cents each	$ 69.95
1000 friends at 10 cents each	$ 99.95
Over 1000 friends:	$ 99.95 plus .05 per friend over 1000.

VISIT http://ObamasDemons.com TO BUY A LICENSE.

http://ObamasDemons.com

CHAPTER 2:

Rules for Discerning of Spirits and Ignatian Pneumato-Ethical Method

In the first chapter I discussed several Bible verses explaining the spiritual gift of discerning of spirits. But before I can try to discern the demons of Barack H. Obama, we must first briefly examine Ignatius of Loyola's *Rules for Discerning of Spirits*, to provide a basis for understanding Ignatian Pneumato-Ethical Method (IPEM), which will allow us to discern the spirits behind our nation's political ethics. For brevity's sake I cannot cover all 22 rules here (which Ignatius numbered "1-14 for the First Week," and "1-8 for the Second Week" of a four-week retreat), which are fully reprinted in the footnote below,[35] for further study. Here I will only cover sufficient ground to introduce my four-step method, also known as my Discerning of Spirits Theological Method (DSTM), which involves 1) consolation-desolation,

---

[35] "Spiritual Exercises of St. Ignatius 313 through 336, From the Literal Translation by Elder Mullan, S.J.," Jesuits Oregon Province, http://www.nwjesuits.org/JesuitSpirituality/Exercises/SpEx313_336.html, last viewed 8 July 2012.

2) consent, 3) manifestation, and 4) pneumato-ethics, each to be explained momentarily.

Church history is replete with examples of this gift of the Holy Spirit, as it operated in the lives of saints, especially Origen,[36] John Cassian,[37] and the three immediate predecessors who most directly influenced Ignatius: Ludolph of Saxony,[38] Jacobus de Voragine (who wrote about St. Dominic and St. Francis),[39] and Thomas À Kempis.[40] A detailed summary of these writers' view of the gift is

---

[36] The importance of Origen's early influence, both ascetically and exegetically, on the early church's understanding of the gift of discerning of spirits is emphasized by Joseph T. Lienhard, "On 'Discernment of Spirits' in the Early Church" *Theological Studies* 41 (1980): 505-529. See also Heinrich Bacht, "Early Monastic Elements in Ignatian Spirituality: Toward Clarifying Some Fundamental Concepts of the Exercises," *Ignatius of Loyola, His Personality and Spiritual Heritage, 1556-1956,* ed. Friedrich Wulf (Institute of Jesuit Sources: St. Louis, 1977), 200-236. See additionally how "Hans Urs von Balthasar has brought together in his anthology of Origen, under the title 'Essence and Division of Spirits,' forty-three such rules 'which anticipate in an astonishing manner the Ignatian Rules of Discernment.'" Urs von Balthasar, *Origenes*, 330-341, cited by Bacht, "Early Monastic Elements," 224.

[37] John Cassian, The Conferences, Ancient Christian Writers: The Works of the Fathers in Translation, vol. 57, trans. Boniface Ramsey (New York: Newman, 1997).

[38] Ludolph of Saxony the Carthusian, Vita Christi: *The Life of Jesus Christ the Redeemer,* cited by Mary Immaculate Bodenstedt, trans., Praying the Life of Christ, First English Translation of the 181 Prayers Concluding the Chapters of the Vita Christi of Ludolphus the Carthusian: the Quintessence of his Devout Meditations on the Life of Christ (Salsburg: James Hogg, 1973); Mary Immaculate Bodenstedt, *The Vita Christi of Ludolphus the Carthusian* (Washington, D.C.: Catholic University of America Press, 1944).

[39] Jacobus de Voragine, *The Golden Legend: Lives of the Saints* (New York: Arno, 1969).

[40] Thomas à Kempis, *Of the Imitation of Christ* (New Kensington, Penn.: Whitaker House, 1981).

provided in my dissertation,[41] which you can read if you really wish to understand the gift as Ignatius did.

Whether you agree with him or not, Ignatius of Loyola (1491-1556 A.D.) is one of the most significant figures in the history of Christian spirituality. As founder of the Society of Jesus (Jesuits), his followers have established over 500 colleges and universities worldwide in the 400 years since his life. Particularly influential are his *Spiritual Exercises*, a set of reflections, meditations, prayers, and mental exercises designed as a model for contemplative prayer, training, and spiritual discernment.[42] Karl Rahner, the globally respected Catholic theologian and admirer of Ignatius, has contended that Ignatius' "relatively brief rules for the discernment of spirits provided a practical and formal systematic method for discovering God's will for an individual…these rules were the first and the only detailed attempt at such a systematic method in the history of Christian spirituality."[43] Another Ignatian analyst, Harvey D. Egan, has stated of Ignatius'

---

[41] Gordon James Klingenschmitt, "Discerning the Spirits in Ecclesial Ethics: Ignatius of Loyola and the Pneumatological Foundations of Ecclesiology," PhD. diss. (Virginia Beach: Regent University, 2012).

[42] Ignatius of Loyola, The Spiritual Exercises of St. Ignatius: Based on Studies in the Language of the Autograph, trans. Louis J. Puhl (Chicago: Loyola University Press, 1951).

[43] Karl Rahner, cited by Harvey D. Egan in Timothy M. Gallagher, "Rules 1–14 for the First Week," *The Discernment of Spirits: An Ignatian Guide for Everyday Living* (New York: Crossroad, 2005), xvi.

Rules for Discerning of Spirits, "His schematization, the concise codification, and the internal structure of his rules contribute to the heritage of Christian spirituality in a way in which no author before or after him has done. They are sui generis."[44]

THREE SOURCES OF HUMAN THOUGHTS

Ignatius told his biographer how he received the gift of discerning of spirits, the supernatural ability to distinguish between the Spirit of God and the devil, as those voices whisper suggestions to his mind:

"They gave [Ignatius] a Life of Christ [The Vita Christi by Ludolph] and a book of the Lives of the Saints [The Golden Legend by Jacobus] in Spanish…in reading the Life of our Lord and the Lives of the Saints, he paused to think and reason with himself. 'Suppose that I should do what St. Francis did, what St. Dominic did?'…he was consoled…one day his eyes were opened a little and he began to wonder at the difference [in his emotions] and to reflect on it, learning from experience that one kind of thoughts left him sad and the other cheerful. Thus, step-by-step, he came to

---

[44] Ibid., xvi.

recognize the difference between the two spirits that moved him, the one being from the evil spirit, the other from God."[45]

Ignatius understood, as did Dominic and Francis, the three sources of our human thoughts: from ourselves, from God (either directly or relayed by messenger angels), or from the devil. The necessity to accurately discern the sources of our human thoughts is a critical element of spiritual discernment. You cannot easily allow God to rule your mind, or evict the devil from your heart, unless you first recognize their voices in your inner thought life. "For the weapons of our warfare are not carnal, but mighty through God to the pulling down of strong holds; Casting down imaginations, and every high thing that exalteth itself against the knowledge of God, and bringing into captivity every thought to the obedience of Christ," (2 Cor. 10:4-5, KJV). Our minds are the place where spiritual battles for our consent take place, between God and Satan.

Ignatius therefore agreed with both the Bible and John Cassian (c.360-430 A.D.), who studied the Bible with disciples of Origen in the Alexandrian school, and wrote:

---

[45] Luis Gonzáles de Cámara, *St. Ignatius' Own Story* (Chicago: Loyola University Press, 1980), 9-10.

XIX.1. Above all we should know what the three sources of our thoughts are: They come from God, from the devil, and from ourselves. They are from God when he deigns to visit us by the illumination of the Holy Spirit...3. And from the devil a whole series of thoughts is born, when he attempts to subvert us both by delight in wickedness and by hidden snares, fraudulently passing off evil things for good with the most subtle finesse and transforming himself for us into an angel of light....4....They also come from us.[46]

The best way to discern between the three sources of our thoughts, and whether they come from us, from God, or from the devil, is to discern their morality. God will always direct you toward moral virtue and holiness, so that you can be holy as God is holy.[47] The devil will always direct you toward immoral vice, so that you can be unholy as the devil is unholy. By the moral agenda of the thoughts, their source is revealed. You or I or Mr. Obama can be led by our thoughts in either direction, either with God or with the devil, to cooperate with right or wrong in every moral decision we make.

---

[46] John Cassian, *The Conferences, Ancient Christian Writers: The Works of the Fathers in Translation,* vol. 57, trans. Boniface Ramsey (New York: Newman, 1997), 57-58.
[47] See Leviticus 20:26; Matt. 5:48; 1 Peter 1:16.

SPIRITS MUST BE DISCERNED BY THEIR MORALITY

Ignatius clearly taught we should discern the spirits especially according to the morality or immorality of their suggestions:

"The enemy of our human nature investigates from every side all our virtues, theological, cardinal, and moral. Where he finds the defenses of eternal salvation weakest and most deficient, there he attacks and tries to take us by storm."[48]

The opening of Ignatius' spiritual eyes, with the new ability to recognize the difference between good and evil spirits which are otherwise invisible to those without the gift, begins by self-examination of the internal and moral movements of one's own soul, which movements Ignatius would later describe in terms of *consolation* (grace from angelic spirits or the Holy Spirit) and *desolation* (temptation from demonic or evil spirits). Ignatius contended that by discerning our own internal ethical movements, we can discern the non-human spirits influencing our human moral thoughts.

Ignatian theologian Karl Rahner agrees that ethics and morals cannot be dismissed as merely human choices,

---

[48] Ignatius, "Rule I:14," *Spiritual Exercises*, 146, emphasis added.

because their rightness or wrongness depends entirely upon the identity of the non-human spirit with whom we consent. After some debate about the subject, Rahner concludes:

"Ignatius' whole system of finding the particular will of God in the concrete would collapse if we were to maintain that it did not matter whether the impulses came from God and his angels or…from concupiscence or from the evil spirit;…It is sufficient to diagnose their moral quality, for that is all that matters…the moral value of the relevant object of choice being recognized from its being inspired by God or the devil. The discernment of its origin is therefore the radical condition of the possibility of distinguishing its moral value."[49]

This quote offers Rahner's strongest possible support for my thesis that ethics and spirits are interdependently connected. The "radical condition" of all ecclesial ethics is discerning their spiritual origin. Unless we discern the spirits, we cannot discern right and wrong, and vice-versa, unless we properly discern right and wrong, we cannot accurately discern the spirits. Thankfully we can learn from those who have properly discerned before us, the writers of

---

[49] Karl Rahner, *The Dynamic Element in the Church,* Quaestiones Disputatae 12 (New York: Herder & Herder, 1964), 163-164, emphasis added.

the New Testament, who provides a basis not only for church ethics, but for discerning of spirits.

CONSOLATION AND DESOLATION

One of Ignatius' first rules of discerning of spirits is to understand the difference between consolation and desolation. As non-human thoughts come toward our minds, how do they make us feel, not emotionally, but morally? Do the thoughts inspire us toward true love, joy, peace, patience, and especially humility? If yes, they come from God, and Ignatius called these thoughts "consolations," which can be so powerful they move us to tears of worship. When you feel moral consolations, these holy thoughts reveal the presence of God's otherwise invisible Spirit. Do your thoughts morally move you toward selfishness, lust, depression, anxiety, anger, and especially pride? If so, they come from the devil, and Ignatius called these "desolations," which can leave us feeling terribly oppressed. He writes:

"Rule I:2. It is characteristic of the evil spirit to harass with anxiety, to afflict with sadness, to raise obstacles backed by fallacious reasonings that disturb the soul. Thus he seeks to prevent the soul from advancing. It is characteristic of the good spirit, however, to give courage and strength, consolations, tears, inspirations, and peace. This He does by making all easy, by removing all obstacles so that the soul goes forward in doing good."[50]

Ignatius clearly defines consolation from God (which influences our human will to choose holiness) as different than desolation from the devil (which influences us to choose sin). Ignatius writes:

"Rule I:3. SPIRITUAL CONSOLATION: I call it consolation when an interior movement is aroused in the soul, by which it is inflamed with love of its Creator and Lord, and as a consequence, can love no creature on the face of the earth for its own sake, but only in the Creator of them all. It is likewise consolation when one sheds tears that move to the love of God whether it be because of sorrow for sins, or because of the sufferings of Christ our Lord, or for any other reason that is immediately directed to the praise and serve of God. Finally, I call consolation every increase of faith, hope, and love, and all interior joy that invites and attracts to what is heavenly and to the salvation of one's soul by filling it with peace and quiet in its Creator and Lord."[51]

---

[50] Ignatius, *Spiritual Exercises*, 141-142.
[51] Ignatius, Spiritual Exercises, 142.

This consolation elevates and inspires our spirit to worship the Spirit of God, and contrasts to:

"Rule I:4. SPIRITUAL DESOLATION. I call desolation what is entirely the opposite of what is described in the third rule, as darkness of soul, turmoil of spirit, inclination to what is low and earthly, restlessness rising from many disturbances and temptations which lead to want of faith, want of hope, want of love. The soul is wholly slothful, tepid, sad, and separated, as it were, from its Creator and Lord. For just as consolation is the opposite of desolation, so the thoughts that spring from consolation are the opposite of those that spring from desolation."[52]

Note how Ignatius lists several particular moral virtues inspired by consolation (inflamed love for God, sorrow for sin, respect for the Cross of Christ, praise to God, increase in faith, hope, love, joy, peace and quiet contentment). Note also how many diverse immoral vices are caused by thoughts of desolation (turmoil, restless anxiety, temptations that cause lack of faith, hope and love; sloth, lukewarmness, depression, separation from God). Do your thoughts promote moral love toward God, or faithless rejection of God? Their morality reveals the identity of the hidden spirits whispering their

---

[52] Ignatius, Spiritual Exercises, 142.

agenda to your mind. If you properly discern the thoughts' virtue or vice, you can accurately discern the spirits.

It can be difficult to distinguish between consolations and desolations when you are in the thick of experiencing them. The devil masquerades as an angel of light,[53] so we often may feel a movement in our soul that is initially joyful but later changes into sin. The lusts of pleasure are often presented to our minds as a deceptive counterfeit of true love; just ask any teenage girl tempted by a boy with selfish ulterior motives. Sometimes suggestions come to us masked as love, but are truly selfish lust. To distinguish false consolations from true consolations, Ignatius clarifies that the beginning, middle and end of the thought must always promote consistent moral holiness:

"Rule II:5. We must carefully observe the whole course of our thoughts. If the beginning and middle and end of the course of thoughts are wholly good and directed to what is entirely right, it is a sign that they are from the good angel. But the course of thoughts suggested to us may terminate in something evil, or distracting, or less good than the soul had formerly proposed to do. Again, it may end in what weakens the soul, or disquiets it; or by destroying the

---

[53] See 2 Cor. 11:14.

peace, tranquility, and quiet which it had before, it may cause disturbance to the soul. These things are a clear sign that the thoughts are proceeding from the evil spirit, the enemy of our progress and eternal salvation."[54]

Here Ignatius offers two clearly ethical criteria as moral indicators of the good and evil spirits, when they suggest thoughts to our minds. Notice in the quote above how the first set of thoughts are "wholly good and directed to what is entirely right." Those conceptions of good and right are essential to any definition of morality, therefore Ignatian discernment is based upon the spirit's morality. Good moral thoughts help reveal to our spiritual eyes the hidden presence of an otherwise invisible angelic spirit. By contrast thoughts from a false angel begin well but it "terminate in something evil, or distracting, or less good…destroying the peace." Sometimes a thought initially appears good, but ends in sin or immorality, so Ignatius concludes the thought must have come from the evil spirit even at its beginning. The moral indicators of "not good" or "not peaceful" are essential to his definition of evil or destructive, confirming Ignatius' ethical construct for discerning an evil spirit.

---

[54] Ignatius, Spiritual Exercises, 148.

The good news is, these thoughts are not necessarily your own, rather they are coming toward you from outside of you, trying to gain your consent. Only after your consent are the demonic thoughts conceived inside of you, but so long as you refuse to consent, the demons remain outside of you, and cannot gain a foothold to your heart or soul. "Each one is tempted when he is carried away and enticed by his own lust. Then when lust has conceived, it gives birth to sin; and when sin is accomplished, it brings forth death," (James 1:14-15, NASB). Temptation is not sin until it is conceived by your own willful consent. You therefore, and not God and not the devil, are fully responsible to control which thoughts you allow to control your own mind. You alone control which spirits you allow to rule your own heart. Their suggestions remain outside your heart until you welcome them inside of you. You have power to invite consolation from God, and resist desolation from Satan, by your own consent to their moral or immoral seeds of thought.

CONSENT

This important factor of our free will was called "consent" by Ignatius, and it defines our human role as we relate to the non-human spirits. Consent is critical to understanding what we choose to do, after the spirits whisper their thoughts to our minds. Ignatius may have learned of the importance of consent from Thomas À Kempis, who wrote about how the devil gains access to our hearts and minds:

"First there comes to the mind a bare thought of evil, then a strong imagination thereof, afterward delight, and an evil motion, and then consent. And so little by little our wicked enemy gets complete entrance, because he is not resisted in the beginning. And the longer a man is slow to resist, so much the weaker does he become daily in himself, and the enemy stronger against him."[55]

Ignatius similarly explains the relationship between these demonic thoughts and human sin, which he defines as consent [of the human will] to carry out evil thoughts [from evil spirits].

"There are two ways of sinning mortally: 1. The first is to consent to the evil thought with the intention of carrying it out, or of doing so if one can. 2. The second way of

---

[55] Ibid., 28, 30.

sinning mortally is actually carrying out the sin to which consent was given."[56]

By adding this important concept of *consent* to temptation (which he distinguishes from *resistance* to temptation), Ignatius establishes how sin includes the necessary human element of willful consent before a binding contract is made with an evil spirit. It is through this contract of the will that permission is granted for the evil spirit to manifest its ethically immoral personality through our human flesh.

Because humans consent to sin voluntarily, we can never claim "the devil made me do it," despite Flip Wilson's comedic claims,[57] or the Son of Sam's tragic excuses.[58] Even if murderers are demon-ruled, the devil is not to blame, and humans are 100% responsible for our own sins. Blame-

---

[56] Ignatius, *Spiritual Exercises*, 18-19.

[57] Flip Wilson, a 1970's comedian, joked about a woman named Geraldine, who told her husband she didn't want to buy this beautiful and expensive dress, but instead she claimed "The Devil Made Me Do It," The Ed Sullivan Show, 11 Jan 1970, https://www.youtube.com/watch?v=0SLifea3NHQ , last viewed 22 Feb 2012.

[58] David Berkowitz, the serial killer known as the Son of Sam, "reported that a dog spoke to him, channeling a 6,000-year-old man named Sam whom he sometimes identified with Sam Carr, a neighbor and dog owner. 'He told me [to kill] through his dog, as he usually does,' David wrote." Steve Fishman, "The Devil in David Berkowitz," New York Magazine, 11 Sep 2006, http://nymag.com/news/crimelaw/20327/index.html, last viewed 22 Feb 2012.

shifting is an unholy diversion that will not excuse us on Judgment Day.

Yet consent is different than willful initiation. Consent is the act of two parties, the human consenting and the non-human spirit to whom our consent is given, whereas willful initiation is the act of one party, you, initiating your own holiness, (as if you could do that without God's help.) We do not initiate human moral holiness (as the heretic Pelagius theorized, but was refuted by Augustine), rather God initiates grace toward us and we consent to allow God to indwell and rule our hearts and become holiness in us. We cannot be holy without God's help.

Conversely, we do not initiate human immoral sin, rather sin comes toward us from outside of us and invades our hearts when we consent to tempting spirits, who indwell and rule our hearts and become sin in us. We are fully to blame for sin, but in practice Ignatius believed we consent to the devil who initiates our temptation. Human sin is therefore always, always, a contract with the demonic. This is why Paul said twice in Romans 7, "I am no longer the one doing it, but sin which dwells in me." We consent to something non-human, every time we sin. That something is a living spirit of sin, which Paul personifies as an intelligent being with an agenda to rule us, and its identity is evil to its core. Paul here teaches that it is not *us doing sin*, rather the spirit of *sin is doing us,* by our voluntary consent to a non-human source.

This element of consent transforms demonic temptation into human sin. Before we consent, sin is not yet human; it is merely temptation outside of us. We need not consent to be tempted, but demonic sin always requires our consent to become human sin. Jesus did not consent, yet he was tempted in every way, just as we are. Jesus was often oppressed by tempting thoughts, but he was not ruled by them, because he did not consent to demonic sin.[59] Let us follow Christ's example, and never consent to demonic temptation.

MANIFESTATION

Unlike Jesus however, we have consented to sin, if we are honest and humbly self-examine our consciences. We must admit we have occasionally allowed evil thoughts to rule our hearts, manifesting a replication of the personalities of evil spirits. "Now the works of the flesh are manifest,

---

[59] See Heb. 4:15.

which are: Adultery, fornication, uncleanness, lasciviousness..." (Gal. 5:19, KJV).

To *manifest* is to be made visible, so when spirits gain access (to work through our flesh) by our willful consent to their suggestions of sin, they enter to manifest through us, and display their moral or immoral personalities revealed by our behavior. The invisible spirits of adultery, fornication, uncleanness, etc. can be seen and are revealed by the works of our flesh. Have you ever looked at another person lustfully? Yes, lets admit we have, so Jesus properly calls us adulterers. Have you ever felt anger toward someone who offended you? Yes we have, so Jesus calls us murderers, revealing the spirits to whom we've given consent in our hearts.[60] Our outer words and deeds reveal the choice of our heart to express immoral vice and contract with the evil spirit behind that vice, expressing its agenda through us like a hand inside a puppet. If we get that demonic hand outside of our hearts, we can cut the strings of demonic control, and regain our freedom to choose holiness and display virtue, allowing the hand of God to work inside us in love, joy, and peace.

You and I have also consented to holiness, and sometimes allowed holy thoughts to rule our hearts, and

---
[60] See Matt. 5:21-30.

manifest (reveal) the personality of the Holy Spirit, through our souls and bodies. Every time you outwardly manifest the fruits of the Spirit of love, joy, peace, patience, and true moral holiness, you are displaying, not your own initiated goodness, but the fruits of the Holy Spirit. God initiated and you consented to allow Him to manifest His holiness through you.

When I see a person's selfless acts of love, I discern the Spirit of God inside them. The Spirit of God is not entirely invisible, but now He is revealed and becomes quite visible as He manifests through your good morality. Just as all immoral human acts are manifestations of evil spirits who work through us by our consent, so too shall all truly moral acts reveal the Holy Spirit manifesting through us by our human consent. The spirits are no longer invisible; they can be discerned through our morality. We can see otherwise invisible non-human spirits, especially God and the devil indwelling human hearts, as they manifest through our outward behavior, and express their personalities through our ethics.

PNEUMATO-ETHICS

Pneumato is an adjective I have derived from the Greek word 'pneuma' which translates in English to the word *spirit*. Ethics involves the study of right and wrong morality. Pneumato-Ethics, therefore, is the term I use to describe discerning non-human spirits according to their moral or immoral characteristics as they influence humans. For example demons tempt humans to sin, so a non-human spirit that immorally tempts us to sin can be spiritually discerned as demonic. Spirits that grace us to choose holiness are good spirits, either angelic or the Holy Spirit of God. When our human friends encourage us to sin (or be holy), they are revealing a manifestation of demons (or the Holy Spirit) in their human behavior.

Spirits can be thus "discerned" in the context of human morality with good spirits revealed by good choices, or immorality with bad choices revealing the bad spirits behind them. Pneumatologically we can study the behavior and characteristics of the non-human spirits through the lens of human ethics. Whenever we see human ethics, either good or bad, they reveal the manifestation of non-human spirits manifesting through the person who has given consent to their good or evil mental suggestions. Pneumato-ethics is therefore the key to discerning the spirits, and this key works consistently, and can be verified objectively, by observing human behavior. This is not some spooky, subjective, opinionated hocus-pocus, where we imagine ghosts that aren't really there, and tell others who cannot verify them. The method proposed here is repeatable, verifiable, and as objectively observable as any human behavior, which can be evaluated biblically, according to the ethically consistent, written standards of morality defined by Jesus and his earliest followers.

THE FOUR STEPS OF IGNATIAN PNEUMATO-ETHICAL METHOD (IPEM):

To recap, the four steps of IPEM are:

1) <u>Consolation-Desolation</u>: The non-human spirit begins *outside* of us, whispering thoughts of good gracious consolation or evil tempting desolation, to persuade the human to consent.[61]

---

[61] Ignatius of Loyola, *The Spiritual Exercises of St. Ignatius: Based on Studies in the Language of the Autograph*, trans. Louis J. Puhl (Chicago: Loyola University Press, 1951), 141-150; Idem. "Letter from Ignatius to Sister Teresa Rejadella (18 June 1536)," 418-421.

2) <u>Consent</u>: After some internal ethical wrestling, the human consents to either holiness or sin.[62] The human is not forced to choose; he or she consents voluntarily, and is thus fully responsible. Consent involves two parties, the human consenting, and non-human to whom consent is given.

3) <u>Manifestation</u>: The non-human spirits move *inside* the human heart, manifesting their good or evil personality and character through the human's ethical action.[63]

4) <u>Pneumato-Ethics</u>: The human ethical behavior of holiness or sin is acted out, as an outward manifestation that reveals the good or evil spirit hidden inside the human heart.

These four steps form an Ignatian method for visual application to the dramatic stage of narrative theology and ethical improvisation, as I have explained elsewhere in detail.[64] For example, whenever we see a human manifesting the evil ethic of pride, we no longer see pride as a mere ethic, but as a spirit of pride. That evil and demonic spirit can be visualized as an intelligent, invisible, spiritual being with a free will, an agenda, and the ability to talk and dialogue with

---

[62] Ignatius, *Spiritual Exercises*, 18-19.
[63] "Now the works of the flesh are manifest, which are: Adultery, fornication, uncleanness, lasciviousness..." (Gal. 5:19, KJV).
[64] See Chapter 4 of my dissertation, named in Footnote 10 above.

the human, first outside during temptation, then inside the human during sin.

Whenever we see a human manifesting the good ethic of courage, we no longer see courage as a mere ethic, but as the Holy Spirit of courage, with a free will, an intelligent agenda, and the ability to dialogue and whisper thoughts, first outside the human during gracious consolation, then after consent inside the human, manifesting holiness. Since the Spirit of Courage indwells the human heart,[65] we know it is not an angel, but the Spirit of God Himself. Since courage is virtue and cowardice is vice, we know the Spirit of Courage is not demonic, but the spirit of fear is demonic.[66] This method enables us to visualize and discern the dialogue of the spirits, revealed by their impact on the ethics of human actors.

Let's now look at three test cases, so you get the idea of how this method can be applied.

---

[65] "For ye are the temple of the living God; as God hath said, I will dwell in them, and walk in them; and I will be their God, and they shall be my people," 2 Cor. 6:16, KJV.

[66] "For God hath not given us the spirit of fear; but of power, and of love, and of a sound mind," 2 Tim. 1:7, KJV.

DISCERNING SPIRITS IN HAMAN AND MORDECAI

Before we examine the demons of Barack H. Obama, it will be helpful to first apply Ignatian Pneumato-Ethical Method to a different political story, so the method itself can be understood. One of the greatest political battles in human history is explained in the Bible in Esther 3:1-6, where we read the historical account of Haman and Mordecai. Haman was an arrogant powerful man who plotted to murder all the Jews in the kingdom. Mordecai was a courageous Jewish prophet who refused to bow at Haman's feet, but rebuked him man-to-man. Their story does not directly mention demons, angels, or the Holy Spirit, but is nonetheless a historical account in which we can attempt to discern non-human spirits revealed by human ethics, using the four steps of IPEM. Picture the scene:

"King Ahasuerus promoted Haman, the son of Hammedatha the Agagite, and advanced him and established his authority over all the princes who were with him. All the king's servants who were at the king's gate bowed down and paid homage to Haman; for so the king had commanded concerning him. But Mordecai neither bowed down nor paid homage. Then the king's servants who were at the king's gate said to Mordecai, "Why are you transgressing the king's command?" Now it was when they had spoken daily to him and he would not listen to them, that they told Haman to see whether Mordecai's reason would stand; for he had told them that he was a Jew. When Haman saw that Mordecai neither bowed down nor paid homage to him, Haman was filled with rage. But he disdained to lay hands on Mordecai alone, for they had told him who the people of Mordecai were; therefore Haman sought to destroy all the Jews, the people of Mordecai, who were throughout the whole kingdom of Ahasuerus," (Esther 3:1-6, NASB).

Note the contrast here. Haman, dressed royally, enters the king's gate, already filled with demons of pride, but not yet filled with demons of rage and murder, outside of him trying to get in. Mordecai, humbly dressed, stands beside the gate, his heart already filled with the Spirit of Courage, but a demon of fear tempts him from outside. The stage is set for conflict between demons and the Spirit of God, which we can see by applying IPEM to examine the morality of the human actors. What non-human spirits manifest in their thoughts, words, and deeds?

<u>Demons of Pride</u>: (spirit manifesting in Haman) "Mordecai, won't you bow to me?"

<u>Demons of Fear</u>: (outside) "Mordecai, he could kill you if you don't bow."

(Ethical wrestling: Fear tries to enter his heart, but Mordecai does not consent to fear.)

<u>Spirit of Courage</u>: (manifest in Mordecai) "I bow before no man; I worship God alone."

<u>Spirit of Peace</u>: (outside) "Haman, resist rage and murder, be at peace, keep self-control."

<u>Demons of Rage, Murder</u>: (outside) "Haman, how dare he disrespect you? Kill him."

(Ethical wrestling: Haman resists peace, Esther 3:5 says "Haman was filled with rage.")

<u>Demons of Rage, Murder</u>: (manifest in Haman) "I will kill all who worship Mordecai's God!"

<u>Spirit of Courage</u>: (manifest in Mordecai) "Do your worst Haman, but God will turn the tables on you."

In this narrative, we can discern the spirits of rage and murder ruling Haman, who failed to discern the spirits tempting him, and let the wrong spirits rule his heart, and manifest through his immoral ethics. If this book were entitled "The Demons of Haman" it would conclude rage and murder were the names of two demons that ruled Haman, simply by objectively observing the moral indicators of

Haman's personal or political ethics. By contrast, we can see in Mordecai the rulership of the spirits of peace and courage, which are manifestations of the Holy Spirit. We see holiness in Mordecai, who properly discerned the spirits giving him grace, and consented to consolations of peace and courage, while resisting desolations of demonic fear and retaliation. Notice the four-step Ignatian method of *consolation-desolation, consent, manifestation, pneumato-ethics* woven into the narrative. From this enhanced narrative, and by applying IPEM principles, we can better visualize the fuller pneumatological drama between spirit and spirit, human and spirit, human and human. Because Ignatian spirits and ethics are connected, we may discern non-human spirits present in every human ethical struggle.

The Biblical text only hints at these spirits, using morally indicative words like "rage…disdain…destroy" (Esther 3:1-6, NASB), and implying "pride" by Haman's insistence on self-exaltation, which terms clearly reveal the human ethics of the story. But with an Ignatian four-step method, we can extrapolate these terms to visualize how Haman's sins progressed: beginning as desolations from evil spirits of destruction outside our hearts, to human consent, to manifestation, to unethical action. The ethical terms reveal otherwise unseen non-human spirits, trying to get into human hearts, and after consent the spirits are suddenly inside of us, manifesting their ethical or unethical personalities through our behavior. Had Haman properly discerned the spirits, he'd likely have made a different ethical choice. Had he seen the Spirit of God upon Mordecai he might have properly assessed his spiritual status, as a prophet before whom Haman should have bowed, rather than self-exalted. But Haman's internal pride prevented him from hearing the voice of humility. His sin prevented his ability to discern the spirits, with negative synergy. Only the truly humble will see the spirits, or properly discern their voice. Mockers in the mainstream media will fail to understand or receive my teaching. This book is not for them. It is for you, the church. But if you are humble, and teachable, this Ignatian pneumatology can allow the narrative to come alive on a multi-dimensional stage, if you are open to receiving the gift to see the non-human spirits interacting within our human ethics.

DISCERNING SPIRITS IN TODAY'S NEWS HEADLINES

You can apply this same method to nearly every story dealing with ethics or right and wrong in tomorrow's newspaper, to discern the spirits working in the human ethics of each news headline. Try to discern the spirits working in these peoples' lives, for example, a recent news story: **"Dunwoody Shooter says 'Angels' Told Him to Kill"**

"Hemy Neuman has already admitted to gunning down the husband of a woman with whom he allegedly had an affair. Now, he's pleading insanity — and saying 'angels' in the form of vintage music stars compelled him to shoot.

"Neuman's defense lawyers insist he was insane when he shot Rusty Sneiderman, a 36-year-old father of two, in broad daylight outside his own son's suburban Atlanta preschool, in November 2010. The defense is arguing that Neuman, bipolar and suffering from psychosis, was visited by a demon sounding like Barry White and an angel with a voice like Olivia Newton-John when he fired and hit Sneiderman three times in the chest at close range in front of Dunwoody Prep."[67]

This story is easy to apply the Ignatian pneumato-Ethical method (IPEM), since the demons (and demons masquerading as angels) are obvious in the shooter's confession. I do not doubt the shooter heard real voices of

---

[67] Scott Stump, "Dunwoody Shooter says 'Angels' Told Him to Kill," Today.com, 22 Feb 2012, http://today.msnbc.msn.com/id/46480036/ns/today-today_people/t/dunwoody-shooter-says-angels-told-him-kill/ , last viewed 22 Feb 2012.

real demons, as he himself claimed. But the shooter failed to properly discern the spirits guiding him. Instead of rejecting the thoughts of desolation and immorality which came toward his mind, he consented to allow those thoughts to rule his mind, and after his consent we see the manifestation of murder, which reveals the demon inside his heart, now pulling the trigger through his body, using him like a puppet. *Even if this person claimed to be a Christian*, (which he did not), we can observe the devil ruling his heart, because it manifest through his behavior. After he consented to the demonic voices, he gave control of his free will to the slavery of sin.

THE HOLY SPIRIT REVEALED IN HUMAN KINDNESS

In other instances, it may be harder to discern the spirits, because they are not directly mentioned in the news story. For example, try to discern the spirits in this story, which does not directly mention the Spirit of God, angels, or the devil:

"Kindness to Family in Sorrow is Overwhelming"

"…The recent passing of my mother, as of any loss in a family, was more than difficult with the gap it created in our lives as well as our hearts. As we all came to mourn her loss on the morning of Jan. 21, the family was all gathered by the funeral director. As he spoke there was not a dry eye in the room; not even his. He informed us that earlier in the morning a lady who did not want her name known came down to make a donation towards the cost of the services. The donation was the entire balance of the services, which as most know is not pocket change by any means. He also shared with us that in 20 years in the business he has never seen anonymous donations more than a few hundred dollars.

The reality of a complete stranger opening up their checkbook to a person they have never met is overwhelming to say the least. Even though the money to cover the cost is greatly appreciated, the generosity and love in ones heart to do such a thing is touching in a way no words could explain. In the manner in which this wonderful woman did this, anonymously, speaks volumes about her character. It shows the love in your heart; not doing good for recognition but just out of the genuine goodness of their heart..."[68]

Although God is not directly mentioned in this story, the otherwise invisible Holy Spirit of Goodness and Kindness

---

[68] Wheeler/Simard Family to Ms. Anonymous, "Neighbors: Thank You Letters. Kindness to Family in Sorrow is Overwhelming," 1 Feb 12, www.telegraphneighbors.com/localnews/948402-147/kindness-to-family-in-sorrow-is-overwhelming.html , last viewed 12 Feb 12.

can be clearly discerned by the human ethics of the anonymous donor. Even common people instinctively know how to discern the Spirit of Kindness ruling in the hearts of other people. The recipient said the donor's kindness "speaks volumes about her character. It shows the love in [her] heart...the genuine goodness of their heart." Since God is love, the recipient saw God in the heart of the donor, manifest in her action of giving. Ignatius would teach that God is seen everywhere love is displayed, especially as He manifests through every act of human kindness. The Bible instructs us how to see the invisible Spirit of God:

"No one has seen God at any time [physically, but] if we love one another, God abides in us, and His love is perfected in us, [and manifests through us, making Him visible]...We have seen and testify that the Father has sent the Son to be the Savior of the world," (1 John 4:12, NASB).

How could the Apostles dare claim to have seen the Father? Because they saw love manifest in the person of Jesus, pneumato-ethically, therefore they saw God in him with their spiritual eyes.

Even if the anonymous funeral donor claimed to be an atheist (which she did not), I would discern the Holy Spirit indwelling her act of love, because God is love. She heard the voice of consolation, the whispered thoughts of kindness, and she consented to those thoughts, and gave generously to a family in sorrow, manifesting the Holy Spirit. We can see the Spirit of God revealed in every human act of true kindness, without exception. Ironically, when atheists purchased billboards asking "Why believe in a god? Just be good for goodness' sake,"[69] they were advocating for the Spirit of God to manifest in peoples' hearts, through moral goodness. They just didn't know how to see God's spirit morally, rather than physically. God is invisible physically, but God is not invisible morally, since His Spirit can be discerned with our spiritual eyes through the lens of true human goodness.

Do you understand now, how the spiritual gift of discerning of spirits can help reveal to your spiritual eyes, the otherwise invisible spirits in every human drama? Whenever the morality (or immorality) and good ethics (or bad ethics) of the human heart are manifest toward good or evil, we can see and hear the spirits whispering to peoples' minds, both before they consent (in consolation and desolation) and after they consent (in their behavior), because their ethics manifest

---

[69] "Why Believe in a God? Ad Campaign Launches on DC buses." Associated Press, 12 Nov 2008. http://www.foxnews.com/story/0,2933,450445,00.html, last viewed 12 Feb 2012.

and reveal the spirit they chose to let rule their heart. This is not rocket science; this is Pneumato-Ethics 101. It's not that hard, but it does require some basic biblical literacy about what is truly moral and truly immoral, as the experts who learned spiritual discernment from Jesus defined right and wrong in the New Testament.

This theological method can be applied to discern the spirits in most other areas of ecclesiology, including soteriology, missiology/evangelism, liturgy, worship, Eucharist, hermeneutics, homiletics, pastoral counseling, church history, and politics. I will need to write several other books to apply IPEM to cover each subject listed here. But since this book applies my Discerning of Spirits Theological Method to American politics, I will now proceed to objectively try to discern the spirits that influence the 44th President of the United States, Barack H. Obama.

We will discover, not only how God has occasionally manifest through his good moral ethics, we will also objectively try to discern the demons that rule his heart.

GET TEN FREE COPIES OF THIS E-BOOK, NOW.

This e-book is available on AMAZON.COM for $2.95 U.S. and other outlets including CreateSpace.com and ObamasDemons.com. This e-book & PDF are copyrighted, and may not be emailed. However, if you purchased this e-book and email to us your e-reccipt, you may obtain a FREE license to distribute the entire PDF of this e-book (as is), to up to 10 friends by email, so this e-book will be FREE for your 10 friends. Register now and email your receipt to license@obamasdemons.com. We will automatically email you a free distributor's license. (FYI, the paperback for $9.95 is not part of this offer.)

GOT A LARGER EMAIL LIST?

You may also purchase a larger license to email this e-book more widely, to more than ten friends, at these rates:

License to email this e-book to:	Cost:
20 extra friends at 50 cents each	$ 9.95
50 extra friends at 40 cents each	$ 19.95
100 extra friends at 30 cents each	$ 29.95
200 friends at 20 cents each	$ 39.95
300 friends at 17 cents each	$ 49.95
500 friends at 14 cents each	$ 69.95
1000 friends at 10 cents each	$ 99.95
Over 1000 friends:	$ 99.95 plus .05 per friend over 1000.

VISIT http://ObamasDemons.com TO BUY A LICENSE.

CHAPTER 3: Barack H. Obama's Demons Revealed (Events 1-25)

THE HOLY SPIRIT REVEALED IN MR. OBAMA'S PERSONAL, RELIGIOUS BELIEFS:

Before we discuss the possibility that President Barack H. Obama is ruled by demons that use him to persecute the church, please allow me to first affirm the possibility that Mr. Obama is ruled by the Holy Spirit of Jesus Christ. Mr. Obama claims publically that he is a Christian, as evidenced by some of his own statements:

In a 2004 interview with The Chicago Sun-Times, [Mr. Obama] said he has "a personal relationship with Jesus Christ" and spoke extensively about his Christian faith. He talked about becoming a churchgoer in 1985 and "[walking] down the aisle of Chicago's United Church of Christ in response of the Rev. Jeremiah Wright's altar call one Sunday morning about 16 years ago." He has spoken of his Christian faith in other interviews and his aides - both before and after the election - have been quoted in numerous publications as saying that Obama has been affiliated with the United Church of Christ since the 1980s.[70]

Clearly from this answer Mr. Obama responded publicly to an altar call, and claims a personal relationship with Jesus Christ. This is no small claim, and appears to reveal the presence of the Holy Spirit ruling in some part of Mr. Obama's heart and character, since the scriptures teach us "no one can say, 'Jesus is Lord,' except by the Holy Spirit," (1 Corinthians 12:3, NASB).

While Mr. Obama's United Church of Christ denomination believes in universal salvation for people of all religions including those who reject Christ, openly endorses homosexuality, and denies the authority of New Testament scriptures such as John 14:6 and John 3:36 which state Jesus is the only way to heaven, members of the UCC do indeed claim the name of Christ, and call themselves Christian. Yet Mr. Obama's own words also clarify why he rejects the authority of scripture, rejects evangelical Christianity, and does not believe himself to be born again. When asked if he were a born-again, Bible believing, evangelical, Mr. Obama

---

[70] Carole Fader, "Fact: The president says he is Christian and no evidence refutes it," The Florida Times Union, 22 May 2010, http://jacksonville.com/news/metro/2010-05-22/story/fact-check-muslim-law-didnt-prompt-michelle-obama-go-home-trip-early, last viewed 29 Mar 2012.

replied to Cathleen Falsani, the religion reporter for the Chicago Sun-Times:

"Gosh, I'm not sure if labels are helpful here because the definition of an evangelical is so loose and subject to so many different interpretations. I came to Christianity through the black church tradition where the line between evangelical and non-evangelical is completely blurred. Nobody knows exactly what it means."

"Does it mean that you feel you've got a personal relationship with Christ the savior? Then that's directly part of the black church experience. Does it mean you're born-again in a classic sense, with all the accoutrements that go along with that, as it's understood by some other tradition? I'm not sure."

Mr. Obama continued his answer: "My faith is complicated by the fact that I didn't grow up in a particular religious tradition. And so what that means is when you come at it as an adult, your brain mediates a lot, and you ask a lot of questions."

"There are aspects of Christian tradition that I'm comfortable with and aspects that I'm not. There are passages of the Bible that make perfect sense to me and others that I go, 'Ya know, I'm not sure about that,'" he said, shrugging and stammering slightly.[71]

Clearly from this answer, in his own words, Mr. Obama is not sure if he is born again. He admits he did not grow up in a particular religious tradition. Certain passages of the Bible do not make sense to him. He is not comfortable with, and therefore rejects the authority of, some aspects of the Christian tradition.

To some extent therefore, Mr. Obama's statement contradicts the teachings of Jesus Christ, who said "Truly, truly, I say to you, unless one is born again he cannot see the kingdom of God," (John 3:3, NASB). He believes he can 'see' the kingdom of God without being born again, or without experiencing what Jesus required. To some extent Mr. Obama contradicts the authority of scripture, which says: "All Scripture is inspired by God and profitable for teaching, for reproof, for correction, for training in righteousness," (2 Tim. 3:16, NASB). Mr. Obama sometimes does not allow the Bible to rule his mind, unless it makes sense to him, therefore his own reason sits in a place of higher moral

---

[71] The Real Clear Politics Blog (Time/CNN) "Obama's Religion," 29 Jan 2007, http://realclearpolitics.blogs.time.com/2007/01/19/obamas-religion/ , last viewed 29 Mar 2012.

authority to him than scripture. At these times he is ruled by his own mind or demons, not the mind of Christ.

The biblical standard for eternal salvation requires far more than merely professing Christ with our lips, since Jesus himself taught "not everyone who says to Me, 'Lord, Lord,' will enter the kingdom of heaven, but he who does the will of My Father who is in heaven will enter. Many will say to Me on that day, 'Lord, Lord, did we not prophesy in Your name, and in Your name cast out demons, and in Your name perform many miracles? And then I will declare to them, 'I never knew you; Depart from Me, you who practice lawlessness," (Matt. 7:21-23, NASB). The jury remains out, therefore, on whether Mr. Obama or you or I are truly saved, despite our confession of Christ as Lord. What do Mr. Obama's words and actions reveal about the moral nature of the spirits ruling his heart?

THE DEMONIC SPIRITS REVEALED IN MR. OBAMA'S MORAL CHOICES:

Having briefly examined Mr. Obama's own words concerning his own religion, we can now turn to examine his policies, and whether Mr. Obama has helped or hurt people of faith and the church. Following is a brief examination of

50 historical events in the Presidency of Barack H. Obama, as recorded by historian David Barton,[72] who cites each event with footnotes and quotes from mainstream news sources. Mr. Barton has not endorsed my theology, nor do I claim he agrees with my theology, although I did obtain his permission to quote from his article which reports 50 historical events. Neither do I claim to be a historian, but as a theologian I will offer my own analysis of each historical event listed by Mr. Barton. I trust Mr. Barton's extensive quotations of original sources including the Washington Post, The Los Angeles Times, NBC, and news articles quoted by Mr. Barton in his 50 observations, listed as follows. By applying my own four-step Ignatian Pneumato-Ethical Method (consolation-desolation, consent, manifestation, pneumato-ethics) to each historical event, we can expose the likely existence and influence of the Demons of Barack H. Obama, and visualize the spirits who influence his ethical conduct.

For example, using Ignatian method, we can objectively discern the spirits tempting Mr. Obama from outside of his person before he consents to do good or evil.

---

[72] David Barton, "America's Most Biblically-Hostile U.S. President," 29 Feb 2012, http://www.wallbuilders.com/LIBissuesArticles.asp?id=106938 , last viewed 29 Mar 2012, used by permission.

After he consents, we may discern the spirit to whom Mr. Obama gave consent, now inside of his person, manifesting through his words and deeds. This theological method allows us to discern the non-human spirits at work behind the events, words, and deeds of the 44th President of the United States.

Each of the 50 Events following begin with a direct quote from Mr. Barton's article. They are each followed by my own analysis of each event, using Ignatian Pneumato-Ethical Method, each concluding with a quote I have selected from scripture.

Now let us discern at least 50 examples of demonic spirits first tempting outside, then ruling inside Mr. Obama.

Event 1. April 2008 – Obama speaks disrespectfully of Christians, saying they "cling to guns or religion" and have an "antipathy to people who aren't like them."[73]

Desolation: Demonic spirits of mockery and disdain (outside, whispering): "Barack, those people who call themselves Christians, they should not cling to religion or self-defense. Go ahead and belittle those who do."

Consolation: Holy Spirit of honor and respect for peoples' rights (outside, whispering): "Barack, the Christian people should cling to God, religion, and have a right to self-defense. Honor their faith and desire to protect their own families."

Consent: Barack H. Obama rejects the Holy Spirit and invites the Demonic spirits of mockery and disdain to manifest inside of himself and through his words.

Manifestation: Demonic spirits of mockery and disdain (acting through Mr. Obama): "I choose to belittle those who cling to God or self-defense."

---

[73] Sarah Pulliam Baily, "Obama: 'They cling to guns or religion'" Christianity Today, April 13, 2008, http://blog.christianitytoday.com/ctliveblog/archives/2008/04/obama_they_clin.html, last viewed 29 Mar 2012, cited by Barton (as are all 50 events cited by Barton).

Pneumato-Ethics: By objective observation of the ethical choices set before Mr. Obama, we can begin to see and discern which hidden spirits whispered good or evil options into his heart and mind. By methodical analysis of Mr. Obama's subsequent choices, words and actions, we can see how he rejected the Holy Spirit and invited demonic spirits of mockery, disdain, and belittling to rule his heart, and manifest through his behavior. *Mr. Obama is ruled, in this instance, by demons of mockery, disdain, and belittling of Christians' religion.* The spirits are no longer invisible, but are fully visible, revealed by the ethics they cause inside the man.

Scripture Mr. Obama Violated: "'For as the waistband clings to the waist of a man, so I made the whole household of Israel and the whole household of Judah cling to Me,' declares the LORD, 'that they might be for Me a people, for renown, for praise and for glory; but they did not listen.'" Jeremiah 13:11, NASB.

Event 2. February 2009 – Obama announces plans to revoke conscience protection for health workers who refuse to participate in medical activities that go against their beliefs, and fully implements the plan in February 2011.[74]

Desolation: Demonic spirits of persecution against Christians (outside, whispering): "Barack, people of faith who oppose abortion should be punished and excluded from government payments, receiving no medical funding unless they cave in, to personally facilitate or perform abortions."

Consolation: Holy Spirit who respects people's conscience (outside, whispering): "Barack, people of faith who are commanded by conscience are also commanded by God, to honor life and not death. Respect their freedom of conscience and do not punish or exclude them because of their inward obedience to God."

Consent: Barack H. Obama rejects the Holy Spirit and invites the demonic spirit to manifest inside of himself and through his policies.

---

[74] Aliza Marcus, "Obama to Lift 'Conscience' Rule for Health Workers," Bloomberg, February 27, 2009, http://www.bloomberg.com/apps/news?pid=newsarchive&sid=a6GWyHUjvpn0 last viewed 29 Mar 2012; Sarah Pulliam Baily, "Obama Admin. Changes Bush 'Conscience' Rule for Health Workers," Christianity Today, February 18, 2011, http://blog.christianitytoday.com/ctpolitics/2011/02/obama_admin_eli.html, last viewed 29 Mar 2012.

Manifestation: Demonic spirits of persecution (acting through Mr. Obama): "I will use the full force of my government to punish Christian health care workers who refuse to facilitate or participate in abortions, by fining them or denying them equal access to funding."

Pneumato-Ethics: The demonic spirits of persecution are no longer invisible, they are revealed by the behavior of the man. His policies, and his enforcement of punishments or exclusions upon those who obey God and conscience, reveal *Mr. Obama is ruled, in this instance, by demons of persecution against Christians, pressuring them to violate their conscience or endure punishment or exclusion.*

Scripture Mr. Obama Violated: "By sinning against the brethren and wounding their conscience when it is weak, you sin against Christ. Therefore, if food causes my brother to stumble, I will never eat meat again, so that I will not cause my brother to stumble." 1 Cor. 8:12-13, NASB.

Event 3. April 2009 – When speaking at Georgetown University, Obama orders that a monogram symbolizing Jesus' name be covered when he is making his speech.[75]

Desolation: Demonic spirits ashamed of Jesus Christ (outside, whispering): "Barack, make sure your staff covers up any religious symbols of Jesus Christ, so you're never photographed or associated with religious symbols during your public speeches."

Consolation: Holy Spirit who magnifies the name of Jesus Christ (outside, whispering): "Barack, surround yourself with staffers who are never ashamed of Jesus Christ or religion, and don't be ashamed to be photographed with people or symbols of religious faith."

Consent: Barack H. Obama rejects the Holy Spirit and invites the demonic spirit to manifest inside of himself and through his words.

Manifestation: Demonic spirits of shame and anti-religion (manifesting through Mr. Obama): "Staffers, make sure you make the Christian University cover up any symbol

---

[75] Jim Lovino, "Jesus Missing From Obama's Georgetown Speech," *NBC Washington*, April 17, 2009, http://www.nbcwashington.com/news/local/Jesus-Missing-From-Obamas-Georgetown-Speech.html, last viewed 29 Mar 2012.

or reference to Jesus Christ, so that nobody will associate me with Christianity when I'm photographed."

<u>Pneumato-Ethics</u>: The Holy Spirit is not revealed by Mr. Obama's ethical choice, rather *demonic spirits of shame and rejection of Christ are revealed by Mr. Obama's choice* to surround himself with staffers whom he instructs to cover up any religious symbols on his stage.

<u>Scripture Mr. Obama Violated</u>: "For whoever is ashamed of Me and My words, the Son of Man will be ashamed of him when He comes in His glory, and the glory of the Father and of the holy angels." Luke 9:26, NASB.

Event 4. May 2009 – Obama declines to host services for the National Prayer Day (a day established by federal law) at the White House.[76]

Desolation: Demonic spirits who reject Judeo-Christian prayer (outside, whispering): "Barack, don't respect the federal law that honors the National Day of Prayer. We don't want to encourage prayer, especially among Christians."

Consolation: Holy Spirit who encourages us to pray without ceasing (outside, whispering): "Barack, it would encourage people of many faiths, especially of the Judeo-Christian tradition, if you would stand publicly and pray, and host a public prayer ceremony for NDOP."

Consent: Barack H. Obama rejects the Holy Spirit and invites the demonic spirit to manifest inside of himself and through his neglect.

Manifestation: Demonic spirits of neglect for prayer (manifesting through Mr. Obama): "Let's not host any public

---

[76] Johanna Neuman, "Obama end Bush-era National Prayer Day Service at White House," *Los Angeles Times*, May 7, 2009, http://latimesblogs.latimes.com/washington/2009/05/obama-cancels-national-prayer-day-service.html, last viewed 29 Mar 2012.

ceremony honoring prayer in the White House, as previous presidents have."

Pneumato-Ethics: Demonic spirits who *neglect or outright reject public expressions of prayer* are revealed by Mr. Obama's actions. The Holy Spirit of prayer is conspicuously absent, and Mr. Obama intentionally neglects to honor Judeo-Christian traditions and the NDOP.

Scripture Mr. Obama Violated: "You have exalted yourself against the Lord of heaven; and they have brought the vessels of His house before you, and you and your nobles...But the God in whose hand are your life-breath and your ways, you have not glorified." Daniel 5:23, NASB.

Event 5. April 2009 – In a deliberate act of disrespect, Obama nominated three pro-abortion ambassadors to the Vatican ; of course, the pro-life Vatican rejected all three.[77]

Desolation: Demonic spirits of death who disrespect the church's views on life (outside, whispering): "Barack, make sure you deliberately and repeatedly send pro-abortion ambassadors to try to embarrass the church and the United States by flaunting our opposition to their views."

Consolation: The Holy Spirit who is the author of the church's view honoring life (outside, whispering): "Barack, even if you personally disagree, you should at least try to honor the views of the Vatican by appointing ambassadors who can understand and appreciate their views on life."

Consent: Barack H. Obama rejects the Holy Spirit and invites the demonic spirit to manifest inside of himself and through his appointments.

Manifestation: Demonic spirits of disrespect for life and the church (manifesting through Mr. Obama): "I will

---

[77] Chris McGreal, "Vatican vetoes Barack Obama's nominees for U.S. Ambassador," *The Guardian*, April 14, 2009, http://www.guardian.co.uk/world/2009/apr/14/vatican-vetoes-obama-nominees-abortion, last viewed 30 Mar 2012.

insist on repeatedly appointing pro-abortion ambassadors to the Vatican, even if they are rejected, because I want to impose my pro-abortion policies on our relationship."

<u>Pneumato-Ethics</u>: The Demonic *spirits of death and disrespect for human life* are revealed in Mr. Obama's choices, appointments, and repeated disrespect for the Vatican's pro-life standards.

<u>Scripture Mr. Obama Violated</u>: "How blessed is the man who does not walk in the counsel of the wicked, Nor stand in the path of sinners, Nor sit in the seat of scoffers! But his delight is in the law of the Lord." Psalm 1:1-2, NASB.

Event 6. October 19, 2010 – Obama begins deliberately omitting the phrase about "the Creator" when quoting the Declaration of Independence – an omission he has made on no less than seven occasions.[78]

Desolation: Demonic spirits who falsify American religious history (outside, whispering): "Barack, make sure you only hire speech writers who falsify or delete religious references to 'the Creator' in historical quotations of America's founding documents. We don't want people thinking they should believe in God as a Creator."

Consolation: Holy Spirit of truth who is our Creator and inspired the Founding Fathers (outside, whispering): "Barack, hire speech writers who are not ashamed of America's religious heritage, and you personally know better, that the Creator should be acknowledged as the source of all true liberty."

Consent: Barack H. Obama rejects the Holy Spirit and invites the demonic spirit to manifest inside of himself and through his hiring and seven speeches.

---

[78] Meredith Jessup, "Obama Continues to Omit 'Creator' From Declaration of Independence," *The Blaze*, October 19, 2010, http://www.theblaze.com/stories/obama-continues-to-omit-creator-from-declaration-of-independence/, last viewed 30 Mar 2012.

Manifestation: Demonic spirits who revise history and deny the Creator (manifesting through Barack H. Obama): "I choose to hire speech writers who delete references to the Creator when I quote from the Declaration of Independence, and I personally misquote our founders documents because I will not acknowledge God as Creator of our liberties."

Pneumato-Ethics: The demonic spirits of *historical revision opposing God as Creator* are revealed by Mr. Obama's staff hiring and his personal speech, repeatedly denying the Creator seven times.

Scripture Mr. Obama Violated: "Remember also your Creator in the days of your youth, before the evil days come and the years draw near when you will say, 'I have no delight in them.'" Ecclesiastes 12:1, NASB.

Event 7. November 2010 – Obama misquotes the National Motto, saying it is "E Pluribus Unum" rather than "In God We Trust" as established by federal law.[79]

Desolation: Demonic spirits that revise American religious history and federal law (outside, whispering): "Barack, you know the national motto acknowledges trust in God, but you should replace that motto with a message about diversity, and deny God any central place in America's principle identity."

Consolation: Holy Spirit who inspires us to acknowledge God's central place in America's principle identity (outside, whispering): "Barack, hire speech writers who are unashamed of God, and feel free to honor God by quoting the national motto, In God We Trust."

Consent: Barack H. Obama rejects the Holy Spirit and invites the demonic spirit to manifest inside of himself and through his speech.

Manifestation: Demonic spirits who revise America's national motto and deny God (manifesting through Mr.

---

[79] Barack H. Obama, "Remarks by the President at the University of Indonesia in Jakarta, Indonesia," *The White House*, November 10, 2010, http://www.whitehouse.gov/the-press-office/2010/11/10/remarks-president-university-indonesia-jakarta-indonesia, last viewed 30 Mar 2012.

Obama's speech): "In the United States, our motto is *E Pluribus Unum* -- out of many, one. *Bhinneka Tunggal Ika* -- unity in diversity. (Applause.)"

<u>Pneumato-Ethics</u>: The Holy Spirit is not audible in Mr. Obama's speech, nor revealed in his heart or mind, since he denies our national motto established by federal law, and refuses to say "In God We Trust." His speech again reveals the *lying spirit of historical revisionism,* ruling his heart, and his speech writers.

<u>Scripture Mr. Obama Violated</u>: "She heeded no voice, She accepted no instruction. She did not trust in the LORD, She did not draw near to her God." Zephaniah 3:2, NASB.

Event 8. January 2011 – After a federal law was passed to transfer a WWI Memorial in the Mojave Desert to private ownership, the U. S. Supreme Court ruled that the cross in the memorial could continue to stand, but the Obama administration refused to allow the land to be transferred as required by law, and refused to allow the cross to be re-erected as ordered by the Court.[80]

<u>Desolation</u>: Demonic spirits that oppose religious expression (outside, whispering): "Barack, make sure you appoint staffers who oppose freedom of religion, even if the Supreme Court says it should be protected. Don't allow Christian symbols anywhere near public viewing."

<u>Consolation</u>: Holy Spirit who encourages freedom of religious expression (outside, whispering): "Barack, never be ashamed of the cross of Jesus Christ. Respect religious freedom, especially for veterans who erect a memorial cross which the Supreme Court allowed, and appoint staffers who will enforce and protect their right to display Christian symbols of freedom."

---

[80] LadyImpactOhio, " Feds sued by Veterans to allow stolen Mojave Desert Cross to be rebuilt," *Red State*, January 14, 2011, http://www.redstate.com/ladyimpactohio/2011/01/14/feds-sued-by-veterans-to-allow-stolen-mojave-desert-cross-to-be-rebuilt/, last viewed 30 Mar 2012.

Consent: Barack H. Obama rejects the Holy Spirit of consolation and invites the demonic spirit of desolation to manifest inside of himself and through his actions.

Manifestation: Demonic spirits who oppose free expression of religious symbols (manifesting in Mr. Obama): "I don't care if the Supreme Court said veterans have a right to display the cross. Make sure my staffers disrespect that decision and ban religious expression in public places. Tear down the cross displayed since W.W.I."

Pneumato-Ethics: The effect of Mr. Obama's actions reveal the demonic anti-Christian spirits ruling his heart, or the hearts of his staffers, who *oppose and forbid the lawful public display of the Cross* of Jesus Christ.

Scripture Mr. Obama Violated: "Do not move the ancient boundary which your fathers have set." Proverbs 22:28, NASB.

Event 9. February 2011 – Although he filled posts in the State Department, for more than two years Obama did not fill the post of religious freedom ambassador, an official that works against religious persecution across the world; he filled it only after heavy pressure from the public and from Congress.[81]

Desolation: Demonic spirits who want to kill Christians and oppose religious freedom around the world (outside, whispering): "Barack, religious freedom is not a priority around the world, so you should delay and avoid appointing an ambassador whose job it is to defend religious freedom in the State Department. Look the other way when Muslims kill Christians."

Consolation: Holy Spirit who inspires religious freedom, especially for the oppressed (outside, whispering): "Barack, my people, the Christians and Jews around the world, face persecution by hostile and angry governments, and my people need a spokesman for freedom. Appoint the

---

[81] Marrianne Medlin, "Amid criticism, President Obama moves to fill vacant religious ambassador post," *Catholic News Agency*, February 9, 2011, http://www.catholicnewsagency.com/news/amid-criticism-president-obama-moves-to-fill-vacant-religious-ambassador-post/, last viewed 30 Mar 2012; Thomas F. Farr, "Undefender of the Faith," *Foreign Policy*, April 5, 2010, http://www.foreignpolicy.com/articles/2010/04/05/undefender_of_the_faith, last viewed 30 Mar 2012.

best person as soon as possible and give them great power to defend religious freedom."

Consent: Barack H. Obama rejects the Holy Spirit and invites the demonic spirit to manifest inside of himself and through his neglect, delay, and lack of appointment.

Manifestation: Demonic spirits who oppose religious freedom (manifesting in Mr. Obama): "Neglect, delay, avoid appointment of a religious freedom ambassador, and only appoint a powerless person after much complaining."

Pneumato-Ethics: The demonic spirits of oppression, neglect, and anti-religious freedom are revealed in the heart of Mr. Obama because of his actions, neglect, and disrespect for religious freedom as a priority for the United States State Department.

Scripture Mr. Obama Violated: "For He has not despised nor abhorred the affliction of the afflicted; Nor has He hidden His face from him; But when he cried to Him for help, He heard." Psalm 22:24, NASB.

Event 10. April 2011 – For the first time in American history, Obama urges passage of a non-discrimination law that does not contain hiring protections for religious groups, forcing religious organizations to hire according to federal mandates without regard to the dictates of their own faith, thus eliminating conscience protection in hiring.[82]

Desolation: Demonic spirits of persecution (outside, whispering): "Barack, you must force Christian employers to violate their conscience, and obstruct their mission to set people free from sin. Instead you must punish Christian employers if they resist your effort to force them to hire homosexual employees who vehemently oppose their religious mission."

Consolation: Holy Spirit of protection for church employers (outside, whispering): "Barack, you must protect people of conscience, especially Christian ministries who are entrusted with a sacred mission, to help educate and deliver people out of sin into holiness. Protect religious exemptions

---

[82] Chris Johnson, "ENDA passage effort renewed with Senate introduction," *Washington Blade*, April 15, 2011, http://www.washingtonblade.com/2011/04/15/enda-passage-effort-renewed-with-senate-introduction/, last viewed 30 Mar 2012.

for hiring by religious groups, so their message is not obstructed or contradicted."

Consent: Barack H. Obama rejects the Holy Spirit and invites the demonic spirit to manifest inside of himself and through his persecution.

Manifestation: Demonic spirits who oppose religious freedom or conscience (manifesting in Mr. Obama): "We will force Christian employers to hire homosexuals that oppose their mission and message, or else we will punish the Christian employers who exercise their conscience, to fine or exclude Christian groups who remain true to their mission of liberating people from sin into holiness. We will label them 'discriminators,' and punish Christians by passing ENDA."

Pneumato-Ethics: Demonic spirits of persecution who wish to destroy the church can be seen in Mr. Obama, who claims to be a Christian yet opposes the Christian message of freedom from sin, which is the Gospel of Jesus Christ.

Scripture Mr. Obama Violated: "Doesn't this discrimination show that your judgments are guided by evil motives? ... Hasn't God chosen the poor in this world to be rich in faith? Aren't they the ones who will inherit the Kingdom he promised to those who love him? But you dishonor the poor!" James 2:4-6, NLT

Event 11. August 2011 – The Obama administration releases its new health care rules that override religious conscience protections for medical workers in the areas of abortion and contraception.[83]

Desolation: Demonic spirits of persecution of the church (outside, whispering): "Barack, force these Christian people to violate their own conscience, facilitate abortions, and distribute abortifacient pills that kill children after they have been conceived. If they refuse to kill children, take away their access to government health care funding, and drive them into bankruptcy."

Consolation: Holy Spirit of respect for conscience and life (outside, whispering): "Barack, your first duty is to obey my command 'Thou shalt not murder.' Even if you refuse, you must never force Christians to violate my commandment, or punish Christians of conscience for their obedience to God, for their refusal to kill children or issue abortion pills that destroy human embryos."

---

[83] Chuck Donovan, "HHS's New Health Guidelines Trample on Conscience," Heritage Foundation, August 2, 2011. http://www.heritage.org/research/reports/2011/08/hhss-new-health-guidelines-trample-on-conscience, last viewed 17 Apr 12.

Consent: Barack H. Obama rejects the Holy Spirit of life and conscience-protection, and invites the demonic spirits of murder and anti-Christian persecution to manifest in his deeds and words.

Manifestation: (Demonic spirit of murder and persecution, acting through Mr. Obama): "The policy of my administration will be to force Christian health care providers to kill children by forcing them to dispense abortifacient drugs, or else face exclusion and punishment and bankruptcy. My government will seize moral control of Christian hospitals to force them into immorality and murder."

Pneumato-Ethics: By objective observation of his ethical choices, we can discern demonic spirits manifesting through Mr. Obama's behavior. *Mr. Obama is ruled, in this instance, by demons of murder and persecution of the Church.* The spirits are no longer invisible, but are fully visible, revealed by the ethics the cause inside the man.

Scripture Mr. Obama Violated: "Men of bloodshed hate the blameless, But the upright are concerned for his life." Proverbs 29:10, NASB.

Event 12. November 2011 – Obama opposes inclusion of President Franklin Roosevelt's famous D-Day Prayer in the WWII Memorial.[84]

Desolation: Demonic spirits of religious oppression that despise public prayer (outside, whispering): "Barack, make sure your staff opposes any public display of religion, especially by veterans groups who wish to display the prayer spoken by President Roosevelt before the D-Day invasion, on the World War II memorial in DC."

Consolation: Holy Spirit of prayer, and freedom of religious expression (outside, whispering): "Barack, only appoint staff who respect and honor freedom of religious expression. Honor and remember the faith and sacrifice of our World War II veterans, and publish the prayer spoken by President Roosevelt in a public memorial."

Consent: Barack H. Obama rejects the Holy Spirit of prayer and invites the demonic spirit of silence and censorship to manifest inside of himself and through his words.

---

[84] Todd Starns, "Obama Administration Opposes FDR Prayer at WWII Memorial," Fox News, November 4, 2011. http://www.foxnews.com/politics/2011/11/04/obama-administration-opposes-fdr-prayer-at-wwii-memorial/?cmpid=NL_FNTopHeadlines_20111104, last viewed 17 Apr 12.

Manifestation: Demonic spirits of religious oppression (acting through Mr. Obama): "My administration will oppose public expressions of religion, and we will block the WWII veterans who have requested FDR's D-Day prayer be engraved to publically acknowledge God's answer to our nation's prayers."

Pneumato-Ethics: By objective observation of his ethical choices, we can discern demonic spirits manifesting through Mr. Obama's behavior. *Mr. Obama is ruled, in this instance, by demons of censorship, ashamed of public religious expression, and dishonoring the memory of our veterans' faith in God.* The spirits are no longer invisible, but are fully visible, revealed by the ethics the cause inside the man.

Scripture Mr. Obama Violated: "Thus the sons of Israel did not remember the LORD their God, who had delivered them from the hands of all their enemies on every side." Judges 8:34, NASB.

Event 13. November 2011 – Unlike previous presidents, Obama studiously avoids any religious references in his Thanksgiving speech.[85]

Desolation: Demonic spirits of unthankfulness and ingratitude toward God (outside, whispering): "Barack, make sure your speech writers honor cultural diversity, and football, and food on Thanksgiving, but don't acknowledge God as the source of provision or blessing. Don't thank God in your Thanksgiving day speech."

Consolation: Holy Spirit of gratitude and thanksgiving (outside, whispering): "Barack, you know all good blessings come from God, and I have blessed you repeatedly. Help Americans remember and honor God first in your Thanksgiving speech."

Consent: Barack H. Obama rejects the Holy Spirit and invites the demonic spirit to manifest inside of himself and through his words.

Manifestation: Demonic spirits of ingratitude toward God (acting through Mr. Obama): "I will honor football,

---

[85] Joel Siegel, "Obama Omits God From Thanksgiving Speech, Riles Critics," ABC News, November 25, 2011. http://abcnews.go.com/Politics/obama-omits-god-thanksgiving-address-riles-critics/story?id=15028644, last viewed 17 Apr 12.

food, and cultural diversity, but I will not give thanks to God as the source of our nation's blessing and prosperity, in my Thanksgiving Day speech."

<u>Pneumato-Ethics</u>: By objective observation of his ethical choices, we can discern demonic spirits manifesting through Mr. Obama's behavior. *Mr. Obama is ruled, in this instance, by demons of ingratitude toward God, ashamedness of God, and lack of honoring God.* The spirits are no longer invisible, but are fully visible, revealed by the ethics the cause inside the man.

<u>Scripture Mr. Obama Violated</u>: "In the last days difficult times will come. For men will be lovers of self, lovers of money, boastful, arrogant, revilers, disobedient...ungrateful, unholy." 2 Tim. 3:1-2, NASB.

Event 14. December 2011 – The Obama administration denigrates other countries' religious beliefs as an obstacle to radical homosexual rights.[86]

Desolation: Demonic spirits of denigration of religious values that oppose homosexual conduct as sin (outside, whispering): "Barack, in your conversation with Hillary Clinton, ensure that you and she directly make speeches which oppose religious values as abnormal, and promote homosexual sin as normal. Then more of your followers will sin, and less will be holy."

Consolation: Holy Spirit of purity and respect for religious teaching (outside, whispering): "Barack, I want people to be holy and pure with their lives, and that means consecrating their sexuality to God, with self-control and faithfulness to marriage. Encourage Hillary to respect peoples' religious values, and encourage sexual purity which betters society for children."

Manifestation: Demonic spirits of denigration (acting through Mr. Obama and Mrs. Clinton): "We oppose religious values that encourage the freedom enjoyed in sexual purity,

---

[86] Hillary Rodham Clinton, "Remarks in Recognition of International Human Rights Day," U.S. Department of State, December 6, 2011. http://www.state.gov/secretary/rm/2011/12/178368.htm, last viewed 17 Apr 12.

because we find sexual purity too oppressive. Instead we promote the demonic oppression caused by homosexual immorality, because we find sin to be liberating, and religion to be despised." (Or to quote Mrs. Clinton precisely: "Likewise with slavery, what was once justified as sanctioned by God is now properly reviled as an unconscionable violation of human rights."[87] Hillary compares sexual purity to slavery, and blames God as the oppressor, as if Hillary's demons liberate humans from God.)

Pneumato-Ethics: By objective observation of his ethical choices, we can discern demonic spirits manifesting through Mr. Obama and Mrs. Clinton's behavior. *Mr. Obama and Mrs. Clinton are ruled, in this instance, by demons of sexual immorality, mockery of religion, and open rebellion against the love that God provides in sexual faithfulness.*

Scripture Mr. Obama Violated: "Although they know the ordinance of God, that those who practice such things are worthy of death, they not only do the same, but also give hearty approval to those who practice them." Romans 1:32, NASB.

---

[87] Ibid.

Event 15. January 2012 – The Obama administration argues that the First Amendment provides no protection for churches and synagogues in hiring their teachers, pastors and rabbis.[88]

Desolation: Demonic spirits of persecution against the church (outside, whispering): "Barack, make sure the lawyers in your Department of Justice oppose religious freedom by churches to hire and fire their own leaders. Instead tell your government lawyers to help sue and bankrupt churches that refuse to hire the government's favored people. Use government power to abolish churches that don't comply."

Consolation: Holy Spirit of religious freedom from government oppression (outside, whispering): "Barack, you know the founding fathers wrote Freedom of Religion into the First Amendment, and your government has no business suing churches or forcing them to hire government-favored leaders. Don't let your lawyers promote injustice."

---

[88] Ted Olson, "Church Wins Firing Case at Supreme Court," Christianity Today, January 11, 2012, http://www.christianitytoday.com/ct/article_print.html?id=94909, last viewed 17 Apr 12.

<u>Consent</u>: Barack H. Obama rejects the Holy Spirit and invites the demonic spirit to manifest inside of himself and through his words.

<u>Manifestation</u>: Demonic spirits of persecution (acting through Mr. Obama): "Make sure, Attorney General Eric Holder, that your lawyers do everything possible to help sue and bankrupt churches that don't hire government-favored ministers, teachers, pastors, and rabbis."

<u>Pneumato-Ethics</u>: By objective observation of his ethical choices, we can discern demonic spirits manifesting through Mr. Obama's behavior. *Mr. Obama is ruled, in this instance, by demons of persecution bent on destruction of the church.* The spirits are no longer invisible, but are fully visible, revealed by the ethics the cause inside the man.

<u>Scripture Mr. Obama Violated</u>: "For the enemy has persecuted my soul; He has crushed my life to the ground; He has made me dwell in dark places, like those who have long been dead." Psalm 143:3, NASB.

http://ObamasDemons.com

Event 16. February 2012 – The Obama administration forgives student loans in exchange for public service, but announces it will no longer forgive student loans if the public service is related to religion.[89]

Desolation: Demonic spirits of anti-Christian discrimination (outside, whispering): "Barack, make sure to punish people of faith, by only paying off the debts of secular community service, but making religious people pay extra for their religious community service. No debt relief for Christians, especially because they serve with community with churches as Christians."

Consolation: Holy Spirit of justice and fairness for people of faith (outside, whispering): "Barack, since Christians pay taxes too, they ought to get equal access to government benefits. Don't discriminate against Christians by withholding benefits because of their religion."

Consent: Barack H. Obama rejects the Holy Spirit of justice and invites the demonic spirit of persecution to manifest inside of himself and through his words.

---

[89] Audrey Hudson, "Obama administration deletes religious service for student loan forgiveness," Human Events, February 15, 2012. http://www.humanevents.com/article.php?id=49551, last viewed 17 Apr 12.

Manifestation: Demonic spirits of anti-Christian discrimination (acting through Mr. Obama): "Persecute the Christian volunteers, by making sure their financial debts are never forgiven, especially if they volunteer at church."

Pneumato-Ethics: By objective observation of his ethical choices, we can discern demonic spirits manifesting through Mr. Obama's behavior. *Mr. Obama is ruled, in this instance, by demons of persecution of Christians because of their faith.* The spirits are no longer invisible, but are fully visible, revealed by the ethics the cause inside the man.

Scripture Mr. Obama Violated: "'A slave is not greater than his master.' If they persecuted Me, they will also persecute you; if they kept My word, they will keep yours also." John 15:20, NASB.

Event 17. Acts of hostility from the Obama-led military toward people of Biblical faith: June 2011 – The Department of Veterans Affairs forbids references to God and Jesus during burial ceremonies at Houston National Cemetery.[90]

Desolation: Demonic spirits of censorship and hostility toward public religion (outside, whispering): "Barack, make sure your Veterans Affairs director forbids and threatens to punish veterans who pray in public, or mention Jesus in their public prayers, or even try to allow Christian burials of Christian soldiers in public cemeteries."

Consolation: Holy Spirit of freedom and religious liberty (outside, whispering): "Barack, don't let anybody work for your government who hates veterans. They've earned the right to freely express their faith in the public square, through prayer in Jesus' name, and especially at Christian burials."

---

[90] "Houston Veterans Claim Censorship of Prayers, Including Ban of 'God' and 'Jesus'," Fox News, June 29, 2011.
http://www.foxnews.com/us/2011/06/29/houston-veterans-claim-censorship-prayers-ban-on-god-and-jesus/ , last viewed 17 Apr 12.

Consent: Barack H. Obama rejects the Holy Spirit and invites the demonic spirit to manifest inside of himself and through his words.

Manifestation: Demonic spirits of censorship and hostility (acting through Mr. Obama): "My veterans affairs staff can oppress Christians, threaten to punish or exclude them if they pray in public, and deny them any right to a Christian ceremony at veterans cemeteries."

Pneumato-Ethics: By objective observation of his ethical choices, we can discern demonic spirits manifesting through Mr. Obama's behavior. *Mr. Obama is ruled, in this instance, by demons of censorship and persecution of the church.* The spirits are no longer invisible, but are fully visible, revealed by the ethics the cause inside the man.

Scripture Mr. Obama Violated: "But you made the Nazirites drink wine, and you commanded the prophets saying, 'You shall not prophesy!'" Amos 2:12, NASB.

Event 18. August 2011 – The Air Force stops teaching the Just War theory to officers in California because the course is taught by chaplains and is based on a philosophy introduced by St. Augustine in the third century AD – a theory long taught by civilized nations across the world (except America).[91]

Desolation: Demonic spirits of anti-Christian censorship (outside, whispering): "Barack, you must re-write world history and political philosophy to secularize all classroom discussion, especially to make our military atheist. Don't let nuclear officers think for themselves, or have any religious conscience."

Consolation: Holy Spirit of justice and religious philosophy (outside, whispering): "Barack, let your military teach about moral conscience, especially the difference between just and unjust war. Don't let your military go to war without moral training, or you'll arm savages."

Consent: Barack H. Obama rejects the Holy Spirit of justice and conscience, and invites the demonic spirit of

---

[91] Jason Ukman, "Air Force suspends ethics course that used Bible passages that train missile launch officers," Washington Post, August 2, 2011. http://www.washingtonpost.com/blogs/checkpoint-washington/post/air-force-suspends-ethics-course-that-used-bible-passages-to-train-missile-launch-officers/2011/08/02/gIQAv6V2pI_blog.html, last viewed 17 Apr 12.

secularization to manifest inside of himself and through his words.

Manifestation: Demonic spirits of anti-Christian censorship (acting through Mr. Obama): "I will not let the military teach just war theory or even discuss any issues of conscience. My officers must never think about right and wrong, they must only obey my will, as if I alone am god."

Pneumato-Ethics: By objective observation of his ethical choices, we can discern demonic spirits manifesting through Mr. Obama's behavior. *Mr. Obama is ruled, in this instance, by demons of tyranny, censorship, and secularization.* The spirits are no longer invisible, but are fully visible, revealed by the ethics the cause inside the man.

Scripture Mr. Obama Violated: "When you draw near to the battle, the priest shall come forward and speak to the people and shall say to them, 'Hear, O Israel, today you are drawing near for battle against your enemies: let not your heart faint. Do not fear or panic or be in dread of them, for the Lord your God is he who goes with you to fight for you against your enemies, to give you the victory.'"
Deuteronomy 20:1-4, ESV.

Event 19. September 2011 – Air Force Chief of Staff prohibits commanders from notifying airmen of programs and services available to them from chaplains.[92]

Desolation: Demonic spirits seeking to silence Christian leaders in the military (outside, whispering): "Barack, we don't want our military to be led by Christians, but it must be completely secularized, so that someday when the anti-Christ leads them, they will obey quickly without considering their conscience."

Consolation: Holy Spirit of freedom of religion (outside, whispering): "Barack, people in the military don't forsake their Christian beliefs when they put on a uniform, neither must they be silent about their beliefs just to get promoted. Let everybody freely talk to chaplains and talk about chaplain programs, regardless of rank."

Consent: Barack H. Obama rejects the Holy Spirit of religious freedom and invites the demonic spirit of anti-Christian oppression to manifest inside of himself and through his words.

---

[92] "Maintaining Government Neutrality Regarding Religion," Department of the Air Force, September 1, 2011. http://forbes.house.gov/UploadedFiles/Gen_Schwartz_Letter_Religion_Neutrali lty.pdf, last viewed 17 Apr 12.

Manifestation: Demonic spirits seeking to silence Christians (acting through Mr. Obama): "Make sure your military leaders promote atheistic silence, and threaten to punish Christian leaders who talk about chapel programs."

Pneumato-Ethics: By objective observation of his ethical choices, we can discern demonic spirits manifesting through Mr. Obama's behavior. *Mr. Obama is ruled, in this instance, by demons of anti-Christian oppression and silencing of Christian leaders.* The spirits are no longer invisible, but are fully visible, revealed by the ethics the cause inside the man.

Scripture Mr. Obama Violated: "The king is not saved by a mighty army; A warrior is not delivered by great strength. A horse is a false hope for victory; Nor does it deliver anyone by its great strength. Behold, the eye of the Lord is on those who fear Him, On those who hope for His lovingkindness…He is our help and our shield." Psalm 33:16-20, NASB.

Event 20. September 2011 – The Army issues guidelines for Walter Reed Medical Center stipulating that "No religious items (i.e. Bibles, reading materials and/or facts) are allowed to be given away or used during a visit."[93]

Desolation: Demonic spirits of hostility toward Christians and Bibles (outside, whispering): "Barack, make sure your veterans hospitals are secularized. No Bibles allowed."

Consolation: Holy Spirit of religious freedom (outside, whispering): "Barack, the Bible is God's Holy Word, and if anybody has earned a right to read the Bible, it is our wounded veterans who sacrificed for everyone to have religious freedom and freedom of the press."

Consent: Barack H. Obama rejects the Holy Spirit and invites the demonic spirit to manifest inside of himself and through his words.

Manifestation: Demonic spirits of hostility (acting through Mr. Obama): "No, my staff at the Veterans Hospital

---

[93] "Wounded, Ill, and Injured Partners in Care Guidelines," Department of the Navy (accessed on February 29, 2012). http://forbes.house.gov/UploadedFiles/WalterReedMemo.pdf, last viewed 17 Apr 12.

should be hostile toward religion, and make written policies that ban Bibles in hospitals."

<u>Pneumato-Ethics</u>: By objective observation of his ethical choices, we can discern demonic spirits manifesting through Mr. Obama's behavior. *Mr. Obama is ruled, in this instance, by demons of hostility toward people of faith, and threaten or persecute Christians who read the Bible.* The spirits are no longer invisible, but are fully visible, revealed by the ethics the cause inside the man.

<u>Scripture Mr. Obama Violated</u>: "I was hungry, and you gave Me *nothing* to eat; I was thirsty, and you gave Me nothing to drink; I was a stranger, and you did not invite Me in; naked, and you did not clothe Me; sick, and in prison, and you did not visit Me.'" Matthew 25:42-43, NASB.

Event 21. November 2011 – The Air Force Academy rescinds support for Operation Christmas Child, a program to send holiday gifts to impoverished children across the world, because the program is run by a Christian charity.[94]

<u>Desolation</u>: Demonic spirits of hostility toward Christian charities (outside, whispering): "Barack, make sure your military leaders and cadets are punished if they talk about Jesus, or volunteer to lead or participate in private charity events. Threaten to punish them of they lead or help religious charities in their spare time."

<u>Consolation</u>: Holy Spirit of charity (outside, whispering): "Barack, my people are commanded by God to love their neighbor, and preach the gospel of Jesus Christ. You dare not forbid them or punish them for doing what God has commanded them to do."

<u>Consent</u>: Barack H. Obama rejects the Holy Spirit and invites the demonic spirit to manifest inside of himself and through his words.

<u>Manifestation</u>: Demonic spirit of anti-Christian persecution (acting through Mr. Obama): "Make sure my

---

[94] "Air Force Academy Backs Away from Christmas Charity," Fox News Radio, November 4, 2011. http://radio.foxnews.com/toddstarnes/top-stories/air-force-academy-backs-away-from-christmas-charity.html, last viewed 17 Apr 12.

military leaders forbid or threaten to punish cadets who participate in chaplain programs, or lead independent Christian programs during their spare time."

<u>Pneumato-Ethics</u>: By objective observation of his ethical choices, we can discern demonic spirits manifesting through Mr. Obama's behavior. *Mr. Obama is ruled, in this instance, by demons of anti-Christian oppression, forbidding or punishing acts of Christian charity.* The spirits are no longer invisible, but are fully visible, revealed by the ethics the cause inside the man.

<u>Scripture Mr. Obama Violated</u>: "Some children were brought to Him so that He might lay His hands on them and pray; and the disciples rebuked them. But Jesus said, 'Let the children alone, and do not hinder them from coming to Me; for the kingdom of heaven belongs to such as these.'" Matthew 19: 13-14, NASB.

Event 22. November 2011 – The Air Force Academy pays $80,000 to add a Stonehenge-like worship center for pagans, druids, witches and Wiccans.[95]

Desolation: Demonic spirits of paganism, witchcraft (outside, whispering): "Barack, although zero cadets at the Air Force Academy claim to practice witchcraft or druidism, you should begin to promote those false religions that nobody practices, and claim it is for diversity."

Consolation: Holy Spirit of worship for God alone (outside, whispering): "Barack, I am the LORD your God, and you shall have no other idols before me."

Consent: Barack H. Obama rejects the Holy Spirit and invites the demonic spirit to manifest inside of himself and through his words.

Manifestation: Demonic spirit of paganism (acting through Mr. Obama): "Let's push these other false religions, and spend tax-dollars promoting them and building for them, even though nobody participates. We'll call it religious

---

[95] Jenny Dean, " Air Force Academy adapts to pagans, druids, witches and Wiccans," Los Angeles Times, November 26, 2011.
http://articles.latimes.com/2011/nov/26/nation/la-na-air-force-pagans-20111127, last viewed 17 Apr 12.

freedom, but really it's idolatry that will someday drag people into hell."

<u>Pneumato-Ethics</u>: By objective observation of his ethical choices, we can discern demonic spirits manifesting through Mr. Obama's behavior. *Mr. Obama is ruled, in this instance, by demons of witchcraft and paganism.* The spirits are no longer invisible, but are fully visible, revealed by the ethics the cause inside the man.

<u>Scripture Mr. Obama Violated</u>: "Asa did good and right in the sight of the LORD his God, for he removed the foreign altars and high places, tore down the sacred pillars, cut down the Asherim, and commanded Judah to seek the LORD God of their fathers and to observe the law and the commandment." 2 Chron. 14:2-4, NASB.

Event 23. February 2012 – The U. S. Military Academy at West Point disinvites three star Army general and decorated war hero Lieutenant General William G. ("Jerry") Boykin (retired) from speaking at an event because he is an outspoken Christian.[96]

Desolation: Demonic spirits of anti-Christian persecution and hostility toward religion (outside, whispering): "Barack, whatever you do, never allow Christian leaders to inspire the next generation of military leaders. Ban Christian generals from speaking at voluntary prayer events."

Consolation: Holy Spirit of leadership (outside, whispering): "Barack, you should encourage Christian leaders to speak freely about their faith at voluntary events, especially to the next generation of military leaders. They must experience true religious freedom before they can defend it for others."

Consent: Barack H. Obama rejects the Holy Spirit and invites the demonic spirit to manifest inside of himself and through his words.

---

[96] Ken Blackwell, "Gen. Boykin Blocked At West Point," cnsnews.com, February 1, 2012. http://cnsnews.com/node/508665, last viewed 17 Apr 12.

Manifestation: Demonic spirit of persecution (acting through Mr. Obama): "My military leaders must discourage and secularize our military, especially by forbidding free speech and Christian inspirational speakers at voluntary events at our military academies."

Pneumato-Ethics: By objective observation of his ethical choices, we can discern demonic spirits manifesting through Mr. Obama's behavior. *Mr. Obama is ruled, in this instance, by demons of anti-Christian oppression, censorship, and hostility.* The spirits are no longer invisible, but are fully visible, revealed by the ethics the cause inside the man.

Scripture Mr. Obama Violated: "Blessed are those who have been persecuted for the sake of righteousness, for theirs is the kingdom of heaven." Matthew 5:10, NASB.

Event 24. February 2012 – The Air Force removes "God" from the patch of Rapid Capabilities Office (the word on the patch was in Latin: Opus Dei).[97]

Desolation: Demonic spirits of anti-religious oppression (outside, whispering): "Barack, even though our national motto is 'In God We Trust' your military leaders should revise and censor any historical reference to God in the military, even on their optionally worn spirit patches."

Consolation: Holy Spirit of freedom to worship and honor God (outside, whispering): "Barack, the people who serve in the military should be free to honor God, even in their artistic patches, which should not be censored, but freely chosen or not chosen to wear."

Consent: Barack H. Obama rejects the Holy Spirit of religious freedom and invites the demonic spirit of secularization and censorship to manifest inside of himself and through his words.

Manifestation: Demonic spirit of anti-Christian oppression (acting through Mr. Obama): "My military

---

[97] Geoff Herbert, "Air Force unit removes 'God' from logo; lawmakers warn of 'dangerous precedent'," Syracuse.com, February 9, 2012. http://www.syracuse.com/news/index.ssf/2012/02/air_force_rco_removes_god_logo_patch.html, last viewed 17 Apr 12.

commanders should secularize and censor any reference to religion or God, even on optionally worn spirit patches. We will not express our national motto. We must not allow trust in Almighty God."

Pneumato-Ethics: By objective observation of his ethical choices, we can discern demonic spirits manifesting through Mr. Obama's behavior. *Mr. Obama is ruled, in this instance, by demons of secularization and censorship.* The spirits are no longer invisible, but are fully visible, revealed by the ethics the cause inside the man.

Scripture Mr. Obama Violated: "Blessed is the nation whose God is the LORD, The people whom He has chosen for His own inheritance." Psalm 33:12, NASB.

Event 25. February 2012 – The Army orders Catholic chaplains not to read a letter to parishioners that their archbishop asked them to read.[98]

Desolation: Demonic spirits of persecution of the church (outside, whispering): "Barack, make sure your Secretary of the Army specifically orders his Catholic or Christian chaplains to remain silent about your pro-abortion policies. If any chaplain reads the letter by their bishop voicing dissent against mandatory church-funded abortions in chapel, threaten to punish them with sedition."

Consolation: Holy Spirit of free religion and prophetic speech (outside, whispering): "Barack, military chaplains are my special prophets that protect freedom of conscience, so that our military leaders know the difference between right and wrong. Let them preach freely against sin."

Consent: Barack H. Obama rejects the Holy Spirit of free speech and invites the demonic spirit of persecution of God's prophets to manifest inside of himself and through his words.

---

[98] Todd Starnes, "Army Silences Catholic Chaplains," Fox News Radio, February 6, 2012. http://radio.foxnews.com/toddstarnes/top-stories/army-silences-catholic-chaplains.html, last viewed 17 Apr 12.

Manifestation: Demonic spirits of persecution (acting through Mr. Obama): "Let the Secretary of the Army threaten Christian chaplains with sedition if they dare preach against the Obama Administration's mandatory abortion programs, now being forced upon Christian or Catholic hospitals nationwide."

Pneumato-Ethics: By objective observation of his ethical choices, we can discern demonic spirits manifesting through Mr. Obama's behavior. *Mr. Obama is ruled, in this instance, by demons of persecution of the prophets in the church.* The spirits are no longer invisible, but are fully visible, revealed by the ethics the cause inside the man.

Scripture Mr. Obama Violated: "You are just like your fathers: You always resist the Holy Spirit! Was there ever a prophet your fathers did not persecute? They even killed those who predicted the coming of the Righteous One." Acts 7:51-52, NIV.

The Score at Halftime: In this chapter, we have applied Ignatian Pneumato-Ethical Method, or Discerning of Spirits Theological Method, to historical events 1 to 25 (of 50) identified by historian David Barton. By applying an objective and repeatable theological method of discernment to several real events in Mr. Obama's Presidency, we have discovered the identities and agendas of following listed names of intelligent non-human spirits manifesting in and through Mr. Obama and his Administration:

Demons of Persecution of the Prophets.

Demons of Tyranny, Secularization and Censorship.

Demons of Anti-Christian Oppression and Hostility.

Demons of Witchcraft, Paganism and Idolatry.

Demons that Forbid or Punish Acts of Christian Charity.

Demons that Threaten or Ban Bible Readers.

Demons that Oppress or Silence Christian Leaders.

Demons bent on Destruction of the Church.

Demons that promote Sexual Immorality.

Demons that openly Mock Religion and People of Faith.

Demons of Defiant Rebellion against Love and Purity.

Demons of Ingratitude toward God.

Demons Ashamed of God, Refusing to Honor, Memorialize, or Acknowledge God.

Demons of Historical Revision who Deny God as Creator.

Demons of Death and Disrespect for Human Life.

Demons who Neglect or Publicly Reject Prayer.

Demons Ashamed of Christ, who Oppose or Forbid the public display of the Cross.

Demons of Lying and Historical Revisionism.

Demons pressuring Christians to Violate their Conscience and Disobey God.

Demons of Mockery, Disdain, and Belittling of Christians' Religious Beliefs.

    This theological method, developed by study of Ignatius of Loyola's *Rules*, reveals the otherwise invisible, evil, non-human, demonic spirits manifesting through Mr. Obama's human words and deeds. The demonic spirits' presence and intelligent agenda are revealed to our spiritual eyes, becoming quite visible when we look at them through the lens of human morality. When we humans consent to their evil suggestions, those spirits invade our hearts and indwell us, and manifest their own immoral character through our human sin. In this case, by examining the immoral actions, words, and deeds of the 44th President of the United States, we have just begun to reveal the hidden demons inside Barack H. Obama. Yet we have much more discerning to do.

http://ObamasDemons.com

GET TEN FREE COPIES OF THIS E-BOOK, NOW.

This e-book is available on AMAZON.COM for $2.95 U.S. and other outlets including CreateSpace.com and ObamasDemons.com.

This e-book & PDF are copyrighted, and may not be emailed.

However, if you purchased this e-book and email to us your e-receipt, you may obtain a FREE license to distribute the entire PDF of this e-book (as is), to up to 10 friends by email, so this e-book will be FREE for your 10 friends. Register now and email your receipt to license@obamasdemons.com. We will automatically email you a free distributor's license.

(FYI, the paperback for $9.95 is not part of this offer.)

GOT A LARGER EMAIL LIST?

You may also purchase a larger license to email this e-book more widely, to more than ten friends, at these rates:

License to email this e-book to:	Cost:
20 extra friends at 50 cents each	$ 9.95
50 extra friends at 40 cents each	$ 19.95
100 extra friends at 30 cents each	$ 29.95
200 friends at 20 cents each	$ 39.95
300 friends at 17 cents each	$ 49.95
500 friends at 14 cents each	$ 69.95
1000 friends at 10 cents each	$ 99.95
Over 1000 friends:	$ 99.95 plus .05 per friend over 1000.

VISIT http://ObamasDemons.com TO BUY A LICENSE.

CHAPTER 4: More of Mr. Obama's Demons Revealed (Events 26-50)

In the previous chapter you saw how I began to apply the four steps of Ignatian Pneumato-Ethical Method, including consolation-desolation, consent, manifestation, and pneumato-ethics, to reveal the hidden non-human spirits that whisper suggestions into all of our human souls, especially in this case the listening ears of Barack H. Obama, to try to influence his moral choices and gain his voluntary consent. Upon gaining our moral consent to choose good or evil, right or wrong, holiness or sin, the non-human spirits move inside our hearts to begin to manifest their own moral or immoral personality through our own words and deeds. Although the Holy Spirit is invisible outside of us, He becomes visible inside of us, and when we choose love, kindness, gentleness, the Holy Spirit manifests through us to display his moral identity for the world to see. "I see the Spirit of God in you," we can proclaim to those who manifest holy love, and it truly is the Spirit of God whom we can see in some people's hearts. However, when certain humans choose selfishness, cruelty, oppression, or tyranny, we can honestly proclaim "I see the demonic in that person," because the otherwise invisible demons become visible when they manifest through human sin.

Using this method we can objectively observe the otherwise invisible non-human spirits, revealed and manifesting through the moral behavior of the human actor. So far we have applied this theological method to historic events 1 to 25 (of 50) in Mr. Obama's Presidency, and by analyzing his words and deeds, we have exposed and revealed some of Mr. Obama's inner demons. Make no mistake, Mr. Obama is fully responsible for his own choices and behavior, but at the same time we can discern the spirits inside of him, and how something entirely non-human has influenced him, entered his soul, and now sits behind his eyes, speaking its non-human words through his human lips. Something "not Mr. Obama" is manifesting through "Mr. Obama." The demons have obtained Mr. Obama's willful consent, and he has voluntarily ceded some degree of control to them, and to that degree they now control him as a cooperative sort of puppet, to act out their agenda, to harm and persecute the Church of Jesus Christ.

This may at first seem shocking to the uninitiated, but your objections to this theological conclusion will be easily overcome with scripture, especially Romans 7 and 1 John 3, if you can try to understand sin as a mutual contract (like a marriage) between the human and the non-human spirit. My point, which may be new to you, is that sin is always, always both human and demonic simultaneously, not just one or the other.

Church history has already established how human holiness is always a mutual contract between the human will and the Holy Spirit, not just one or the other. Augustine proved this when refuting Pelagius,[99] who believed humans could be holy without God's spirit of grace, when in truth we never do initiate human holiness except in response to God's initial gracious influence toward our hearts. If you deny this, you believe the Pelagian heresy that promotes humanism, and you reject the Augustinian orthodoxy of Christianity.

Additionally I'm now saying (and successfully defended from scripture in my PhD dissertation defense), that the inverse is also true, that if humans are not independently holy, then neither are we independently sinful. Human sin

---

[99] "No one lives rightly without the grace of God." Augustine, "On the Proceedings of Pelagius," *The Fathers of the Church: A New Translation,* vol. 86 (Washington D.C.: Catholic University of America Press, 1992), 113.

always opens the door and gives a foothold to a voluntary and mutual contract with a non-human demonic spirit,[100] and that demon is given permission to manifest its evil personality through our human behavior. Of course Mr. Obama remains fully human, but something manifesting through him is non-human, to which he has voluntarily ceded some degree of control.

That is why Paul repeats twice in Romans 7:17,19 (NASB): "no longer am I the one doing it, but sin which dwells in me," and "I am no longer the one doing it, but sin which dwells in me." Or in other words, every time Paul, or Mr. Obama, (or you or I) consent to sin, there is something "not Paul" or "not Mr. Obama" or "not human" inside of him doing the work. If you deny this, and say sin is entirely human, or "that is only Paul," or "that is only Mr. Obama," then you deny the scriptures. Paul says twice "I am no longer the one doing it." Something non-human indwells Paul's human flesh here. You believe a humanist heresy if you interpret this to mean "Paul is the only one doing it," when Paul himself clearly twice said the opposite. You reject the Bible if you believe Paul sinned alone, since Paul himself teaches "I am no longer the one doing it." Human sin

---

[100] See Ephesians 4:27.

therefore contains a non-human element to its being, in some way. Sin has its own intellect, will, and an agenda to take over our bodies and manifest its evil and non-human personality through our human body. Sin is "not Paul" and therefore "not human." Sin is demonic.

False teachers and humanists will try to argue sin is not really demonic, and it's entirely human, but they must also ignore 1 John 3:8, 10, (NASB): "the one who practices sin is of the devil; for the devil has sinned from the beginning...By this the children of God and the children of the devil are obvious: anyone who does not practice righteousness is not of God..." So again I say, human sin is always, always demonic simultaneously, by our voluntary human cooperation with evil non-human spirits. If you are engaged in sin, scripture says you are "of the devil," and a "child of the devil." You believe a humanist heresy if you deny this, and try to claim the opposite, that humans can sin freely without demonic involvement, since your view is anti-Biblical and claims humans who sin are "not of the devil," or "not a child of the devil." Your interpretation intentionally promotes the exact opposite of what scripture plainly says. The Biblical truth is that human sin always, always gives the devil a foothold in our soul (Eph 4:27), and invites a manifestation of evil non-human spirits, who gain our consent to rule our hearts, so they can display their immorality through us with our voluntary consent. The invisible spirits are thus made visible, and can be plainly seen by any objective observers, if they look through the revealing lens of human morality. Good human morals reveal the Holy Spirit inside of us. Bad human immorality reveals demonic spirits working through their human cooperators. The Ignatian method allows us to discern non-human spirits revealed in human ethics.

This leads to an uncomfortable conclusion, if we take the scriptures literally on this point. Mr. Obama (or Paul or you and I) may need an occasional exorcism, (if that's true then it's true regardless of how it makes us feel), or maybe he simply needs to repent in private, and the Holy Spirit will evict the demon when he's alone, but either way the demon is really there, and it really would depart if he (or Paul or you or I) truly repented. Mr. Obama, to the exact degree to which his actions are voluntarily sinful, is voluntarily controlled by demonic spirits. He cooperates with them, manifests them, and they are no longer invisible, we can see the evil spirits revealed by his immoral acts. This book is not mis-titled; it really does reveal the inner demons of Barack H. Obama.

Perhaps somebody will hand Mr. Obama this book, and he will consider some spiritual self-examination (as I do daily), but until then let us continue to analyze the historic events of his Presidency, numbered 26 to 50.

Historian David Barton,[101] who has not endorsed my theology nor do I claim his endorsement, directly quotes objective news sources including whitehouse.gov, ABC and CBS News, CNN, the New York Times, and the Washington Post, among others. Again my goal here is not to act as historian, but to trust the unbiased historicity of events as already reported by others, and now specifically apply my own unique theological method, following the tradition of Ignatius of Loyola's *Rules for the Discerning of Spirits*. By objectively applying this theological method, we can begin to see and visualize the otherwise invisible non-human spirits, as they whisper to enter and manifest through the human, in this case the 44th President of the United States.

Completing Mr. Barton's top 50 anti-Christian events of the Obama Presidency, 26 to 50:

---

[101] David Barton, "America's Most Biblically-Hostile U.S. President," 29 Feb 12, http://www.wallbuilders.com/LIBissuesArticles.asp?id=106938#FN14, last viewed 17 Apr 12, used by permission.

Event 26. January 2009 – Obama lifts restrictions on U.S. government funding for groups that provide abortion services or counseling abroad, forcing taxpayers to fund pro-abortion groups that either promote or perform abortions in other nations – President Obama's nominee for deputy secretary of state asserts that American taxpayers are required to pay for abortions and that limits on abortion funding are unconstitutional.[102]

Desolation: Demonic spirits of death, murder (outside, whispering): "Barack, if you lift these restrictions on funding abortion with tax-payer dollars, you can increase the number of murders of children of poor people, and further legalize and even subsidize what God has forbidden, the slaughter of innocents."

Consolation: Holy Spirit of life (outside, whispering): "Barack, you should use the power of your office to protect innocent life, especially helpless children in the womb, because every child is cherished and destined by God with

---

[102] Jeff Mason and Deborah Charles, "Obama lifts restrictions on abortion funding," Reuters, January 23, 2009, http://www.reuters.com/article/2009/01/23/us-obama-abortion-idUSTRE50M3PQ20090123, last viewed 17 Apr 12; "Obama pick: Taxpayers must fund abortions," World Net Daily, January 27, 2009. http://www.wnd.com/2009/01/87249/, last viewed 17 Apr 12.

the inalienable right to life. Cease funding abortion providers with tax-dollars."

Consent: Barack H. Obama rejects the Holy Spirit and invites the demonic spirit to manifest inside of himself and through his words.

Manifestation: (Demonic spirit acting through Mr. Obama): "I demand government funding of Planned Parenthood and other abortion providers with our tax-payer dollars. I will subsidize child-murder in the name of 'health' care."

Pneumato-Ethics: By objective observation of his ethical choices, we can discern demonic spirits manifesting through Mr. Obama's behavior. *Mr. Obama is ruled, in this instance, by demons of death and murder.* The spirits are no longer invisible, but are fully visible, revealed by the ethics they help cause inside the man who promotes sin.

Scripture Mr. Obama Violated:
"Thou shalt not murder." Exodus 20:13, NASB.

Event 27. March 2009 – The Obama administration shut out pro-life groups from attending a White House-sponsored health care summit.[103]

Desolation: Demonic spirits of death and persecution (outside, whispering): "Barack, make sure your staffers exclude and persecute Christian groups who refuse to participate in abortions, by denying them access to government training and government funding for their healthcare programs. Make them pledge to kill children if they want access to 'health' care funding."

Consolation: Holy Spirit of life (outside, whispering): "Barack, never force Christian health care workers to kill children as a price of admission to equal access to government programs and benefits. In fact you should immediately withdraw all government support for child-murderers, and refuse to fund them unless they stand for life, and keep their Hippocratic oath to 'first do no harm.'"

Consent: Barack H. Obama rejects the Holy Spirit and invites the demonic spirit to manifest inside of himself and through his words.

---

[103] Steven Ertelt, "Pro-Life Groups Left Off Obama's Health Care Summit List, Abortion Advocates OK," LifeNews, March 5, 2009. http://www.lifenews.com/2009/03/05/nat-4888/, last viewed 17 Apr 12.

Manifestation: (Demonic spirit acting through Mr. Obama): "I will use the power of my office to exclude and persecute Christians who refuse to kill innocent children or participate in abortion, by denying them access to government benefits and 'health' care benefits."

<u>Pneumato-Ethics</u>: By objective observation of his ethical choices, we can discern demonic spirits manifesting through Mr. Obama's behavior. *Mr. Obama is ruled, in this instance, by demons of death and persecution.* The spirits are no longer invisible, but are fully visible, revealed by the ethics they help cause inside the man who promotes sin.

<u>Scripture Mr. Obama Violated</u>: "Many are the foes who persecute me, but I have not turned from your statutes…Rulers persecute me without cause, but my heart trembles at your word." Psalm 119:157,161, NASB.

Event 28. March 2009 – Obama orders taxpayer funding of embryonic stem cell research.[104]

Desolation: Demonic spirits of death and child-murder (outside, whispering): "Barack, re-define medical 'ethics' to require the slaughter of children conceived in the laboratory, and subsidize the unnecessary creation of more children in labs, so their body parts can be destroyed or used in stem-cell experiments that benefit the child-murderers."

Consolation: Holy Spirit of life (outside, whispering): "Barack, human life medically begins at conception, so you must take extreme care to only subsidize and allow truly ethical doctors that never create babies for the sole purpose of destruction or experimentation. If a baby will not be implanted and given the opportunity to grow, it should never be created in the first place."

Consent: Barack H. Obama rejects the Holy Spirit and invites the demonic spirit to manifest inside of himself and through his words.

---

[104] "Obama Signs Order Lifting Restrictions on Stem Cell Research Funding," Fox News, March 9, 2009. http://www.foxnews.com/politics/2009/03/09/obama-signs-order-lifting-restrictions-stem-cell-research-funding/, last viewed 17 Apr 12.

Manifestation: (Demonic spirit acting through Mr. Obama): "I order the government-funded unethical destruction of children in embryo form, and the government-funded creation of more children so their body parts can be harvested for experiments or to benefit their child-murderers."

Pneumato-Ethics: By objective observation of his ethical choices, we can discern demonic spirits manifesting through Mr. Obama's behavior. *Mr. Obama is ruled, in this instance, by demons of death and child-murder.* The spirits are no longer invisible, but are fully visible, revealed by the ethics they help cause inside the man who promotes sin.

Scripture Mr. Obama Violated: "Do not put an innocent or honest person to death, for I will not acquit the guilty." Exodus 23:7, NASB.

Event 29. March 2009 – Obama gave $50 million for the UNFPA, the UN population agency that promotes abortion and works closely with Chinese population control officials who use forced abortions and involuntary sterilizations.[105]

Desolation: Demonic spirits of worldwide child-murder (outside, whispering): "Barack, it's not enough that your government funds murder and kills American children. Send American tax-payer dollars to the United Nations to fund and subsidize the slaughter of foreign children too."

Consolation: Holy Spirit of life and love for neighbor (outside, whispering): "Barack, if you obey Christ's command to love your neighbor, you will never allow tax-payer funding to slaughter innocent foreign children, and you will never subsidize or fund Chinese programs that force unwilling women to abort their own children against their will."

---

[105] Steven Ertelt, "President Barack Obama's Pro-Abortion Record: A Pro-Life Compilation," LifeNews, February 11, 2012, http://www.lifenews.com/2010/11/07/obamaabortionrecord/, last viewed 17 Apr 12.

Consent: Barack H. Obama rejects the Holy Spirit and invites the demonic spirit to manifest inside of himself and through his words.

Manifestation: (Demonic spirit acting through Mr. Obama): "In the false name of population control, I demand we send $50 million of American tax-payer dollars to fund mandatory abortions and child-murder of Chinese babies against the will of their own mothers."

Pneumato-Ethics: By objective observation of his ethical choices, we can discern demonic spirits manifesting through Mr. Obama's behavior. *Mr. Obama is ruled, in this instance, by demons of tyranny, death, and child-murder.* The spirits are no longer invisible, but are fully visible, revealed by the ethics they help cause inside the man who promotes sin.

Scripture Mr. Obama Violated: "There are six things which the LORD hates, yes, seven which are an abomination to Him: Haughty eyes, a lying tongue, and hands that shed innocent blood…" Proverbs 6:16-17, NASB.

Event 30. May 2009 – The White House budget eliminates all funding for abstinence-only education and replaces it with comprehensive sexual education, repeatedly proven to increase teen pregnancies and abortions. He continues the deletion in subsequent budgets.[106]

Desolation: Demonic spirits of sexual immorality and child-perversion (outside, whispering): "Barack, please stop any government funding of sex-education of teens that promotes abstinence until marriage, and instead use tax-payer dollars to promote sexual immorality among teens, to promote more sexual immorality, and more teen abortions using post-conception abortion pills."

Consolation: Holy Spirit of self-control and sexual purity (outside, whispering): "Barack, God created sex only for marriage between one man and one woman, not for unmarried teens, so your government educators should help parents promote abstinence among teens, to prevent sexual immorality and teen pregnancy."

---

[106] Steven Ertelt, "Barack Obama's Federal Budget Eliminates Funding for Abstinence-Only Education," LifeNews, May 8, 2009. http://www.lifenews.com/2009/05/08/nat-5032/, last viewed 17 Apr 12; Steven Ertelt, "Obama Budget Funds Sex Ed Over Abstinence on 16-1 Margin," LifeNews, February 14, 2011. http://www.lifenews.com/2011/02/14/new-obama-budget-funds-sex-ed-over-abstinence-on-16-1-margin/, last viewed 17 Apr 12.

Consent: Barack H. Obama rejects the Holy Spirit and invites the demonic spirit to manifest inside of himself and through his words.

Manifestation: (Demonic spirit acting through Mr. Obama): "Teens should have more sex and more abortions, not less, so I order government funding of sex-education that ignores abstinence and promotes teen sexual immorality and abortion pills."

Pneumato-Ethics: By objective observation of his ethical choices, we can discern demonic spirits manifesting through Mr. Obama's behavior. *Mr. Obama is ruled, in this instance, by demons of sexual immorality and child-perversion.* The spirits are no longer invisible, but are fully visible, revealed by the ethics they help cause inside the man who promotes sin who promotes sin.

Scripture Mr. Obama Violated: "It would be better for him to be thrown into the sea with a millstone tied around his neck than for him to cause one of these little ones to sin." Luke 17:2, NIV.

Event 31. May 2009 – Obama officials assemble a terrorism dictionary calling pro-life advocates violent and charging that they use racism in their 'criminal' activities.[107]

Desolation: Demonic spirits of deception and false accusation (outside, whispering): "Barack, make sure your homeland defense staff labels Christians as 'terrorists' and pro-lifers as 'pro-violence' even if they peacefully protest your government-funded murder of unborn children."

Consolation: Holy Spirit of truth and prophetic utterance (outside, whispering): "Barack, do you see those pro-lifers in the street peacefully speaking truth? I the Holy Spirit speak to you through them, and I call you to repent of your child-murder by funding abortion. Do not persecute my prophets, but listen to their truth and stop your own sin."

Consent: Barack H. Obama rejects the Holy Spirit and invites the demonic spirit to manifest inside of himself and through his words.

Manifestation: (Demonic spirit acting through Mr. Obama): "Instead of listening to the truth spoken by peaceful pro-life protestors, I will persecute them by labeling them

---

[107] Steven Ertelt, "Obama Admin Terrorism Dictionary Calls Pro-Life Advocates Violent, Racist," LifeNews, May 5, 2009. http://www.lifenews.com/2009/05/05/nat-5019/, last viewed 17 Apr 12.

'terrorists' and training my homeland security people to view Christian citizens as the enemy."

<u>Pneumato-Ethics</u>: By objective observation of his ethical choices, we can discern demonic spirits manifesting through Mr. Obama's behavior. *Mr. Obama is ruled, in this instance, by demons of deception and false accusation.* The spirits are no longer invisible, but are fully visible, revealed by the ethics they help cause inside the man who promotes sin.

<u>Scripture Mr. Obama Violated</u>: "Your tongue devises destruction, Like a sharp razor, O worker of deceit. You love evil more than good, Falsehood more than speaking what is right. You love all words that devour, O deceitful tongue." Psalm 52:2-4, NASB.

Event 32. July 2009 – The Obama administration illegally extends federal benefits to same-sex partners of Foreign Service and Executive Branch employees, in direction violation of the federal Defense of Marriage Act.[108]

Desolation: Demonic spirits of homosexuality, lust and sexual immorality (outside, whispering): "Barack, if you give government benefits and bonus pay to those who commit immoral sexual acts, you will reward their sin, and entice more people to sin sexually, by offering a government endorsement of their immoral behavior. If you re-label wrong as right, and lust as love, you can confuse and re-educate the public, dragging many more people into rebellion against God's law."

Consolation: Holy Spirit of purity and love (outside, whispering): "Barack, love is about selfless sacrifice, but lust is about selfish pleasure. Do not reward sexual immorality of any kind with extra government bonus pay, but let your government reflect God's government, so that it rewards

---

[108] "Memorandum for the Heads of Executive Departments and Agencies," The White House, June 17, 2009.
http://www.whitehouse.gov/the_press_office/Memorandum-for-the-Heads-of-Executive-Departments-and-Agencies-on-Federal-Benefits-and-Non-Discrimination-6-17-09/, last viewed 17 Apr 12.

sacrificial love and punishes selfish lust, just like God will do on judgment day."

Consent: Barack H. Obama rejects the Holy Spirit and invites the demonic spirit to manifest inside of himself and through his words.

Manifestation: (Demonic spirit acting through Mr. Obama): "My government will reward and issue bonus pay to people who engage in sexual immorality, to reward their sin and confuse the public about right and wrong. My government is smarter than God's government."

Pneumato-Ethics: By objective observation of his ethical choices, we can discern demonic spirits manifesting through Mr. Obama's behavior. *Mr. Obama is ruled, in this instance, by demons of sexual immorality and homosexual lust.* The spirits are no longer invisible, but are fully visible, revealed by the ethics they help cause inside the man who promotes sin.

Scripture Mr. Obama Violated: "Do you not know that the unrighteous will not inherit the kingdom of God? Do not be deceived; neither fornicators, nor idolaters, nor adulterers, nor effeminate, nor homosexuals, nor thieves, nor the covetous, nor drunkards, nor revilers, nor swindlers, will inherit the kingdom of God." 1 Cor. 6:9-10, NASB.

Event 33. September 16, 2009 – The Obama administration appoints as EEOC Commissioner Chai Feldblum, who asserts that society should "not tolerate" any "private beliefs," including religious beliefs, if they may negatively affect homosexual "equality."[109]

Desolation: Demonic spirits of persecution and sexual immorality (outside, whispering): "Barack, please help me deceive people into thinking love is hate, lust is love, and truth is intolerant. Whenever a Christian business-owner speaks publicly against sin, punish and persecute them by seizing their business, fine them, make them liable to lawsuits, force religious people to hire and promote immorality. Favor tolerance of sin over religious freedom."

Consolation: Holy Spirit of truth and purity (outside, whispering): "Barack, don't discriminate against Christians who promote truth, or punish employers who hold to sincere Christian standards of hiring and promotion. Protect Christian churches, bookstores, schools, and religious employers freedom to hire sexually pure role models to

---

[109] Matt Cover, "Obama's EEOC Nominee: Society Should 'Not Tolerate Private Beliefs' That 'Adversely Affect' Homosexuals," cnsnews.com, January 18, 2010. http://cnsnews.com/node/59965, last viewed 17 Apr 12.

promote their religious mission. Tolerate Christian truth, not sexual immorality."

Consent: Barack H. Obama rejects the Holy Spirit and invites the demonic spirit to manifest inside of himself and through his words.

Manifestation: (Demonic spirit acting through Mr. Obama): "In the name of false tolerance, my EEOC will not tolerate Christian truth, and we will punish Christian employers and organizations whose religious mission requires they uphold moral standards for hiring or promotion."

Pneumato-Ethics: By objective observation of his ethical choices, we can discern demonic spirits manifesting through Mr. Obama's behavior. *Mr. Obama is ruled, in this instance, by demons of persecution and sexual immorality.*

Scripture Mr. Obama Violated: "With all the deception of wickedness for those who perish, because they did not receive the love of the truth so as to be saved. For this reason God will send upon them a deluding influence so that they will believe what is false, in order that they all may be judged who did not believe the truth, but took pleasure in wickedness." 2 Thess. 2:10-12.

Event 34. July 2010 – The Obama administration uses federal funds in violation of federal law to get Kenya to change its constitution to include abortion.[110]

<u>Desolation</u>: Demonic spirits of genocide, child-murder and tyranny (outside, whispering): "Barack, use your power to force other nations to promote and fund abortion and child-murder. Give money to reward nations who promote child-murder, and withhold money from nations that prevent abortion. Arm-twist Kenya to change their laws to promote child-murder of the unborn."

<u>Consolation</u>: Holy Spirit of life and service to others (outside, whispering): "Barack, use the power of your office to serve other nations, not rule them with tyranny. Never reward evil, and only reward good. Send money to nations who protect innocent life, not to child-murderers."

<u>Consent</u>: Barack H. Obama rejects the Holy Spirit and invites the demonic spirit to manifest inside of himself and through his words.

---

[110] Tess Civantos, "White House Spent $23M of Taxpayer Money to Back Kenyan Constitution That Legalizes Abortion, GOP Reps Say," Fox News, July 22, 2010. http://www.foxnews.com/politics/2010/07/21/gop-lawmaker-blasts-white-house-m-spent-kenya-constitution-vote/, last viewed 17 Apr 12.

Manifestation: (Demonic spirit acting through Mr. Obama): "I will violate federal law that forbids use of taxpayer dollars to subsidize foreign abortions to bribe and reward the Kenyan government to promote child-murder in their Constitution, killing untold thousands of future babies in government-sanctioned genocide against the unborn."

Pneumato-Ethics: By objective observation of his ethical choices, we can discern demonic spirits manifesting through Mr. Obama's behavior. *Mr. Obama is ruled, in this instance, by demons of genocide, child-murder, and tyranny.* The spirits are no longer invisible, but are fully visible, revealed by the ethics they help cause inside the man who promotes sin.

Scripture Mr. Obama Violated: "He became very enraged, and sent and slew all the male children who were in Bethlehem and all its vicinity…Then what had been spoken through Jeremiah the prophet was fulfilled:

'A voice was heard in Ramah,

weeping and great mourning,

Rachel weeping for her children;

and she refused to be comforted,

because they were no more.' "

Matthew 2:16-18, NASB.

Event 35. August 2010 – The Obama administration Cuts funding for 176 abstinence education programs.[111]

Desolation: Demonic spirits of sexual immorality and deception (outside, whispering): "Barack, use the power of your office to promote sexual immorality in public schools, so teens will not learn the benefits of sexual purity and abstinence, causing more sexual sin and teen pregnancy, which often leads to more abortion and more child-murder."

Consolation: Holy Spirit of purity, love, and respect for life (outside, whispering): "Barack, parents need support from school teachers to promote sexual purity among teens, and abstinence until marriage, which prevents teen pregnancy and promotes true patience and love. True love waits to have sex until marriage, and avoids selfish lust."

Consent: Barack H. Obama rejects the Holy Spirit and invites the demonic spirit to manifest inside of himself and through his words.

Manifestation: (Demonic spirit acting through Mr. Obama): "My government will de-fund abstinence based education and oppose parents efforts to prevent teen

---

[111] Steven Ertelt, "Obama, Congress Cut Funding for 176 Abstinence Programs Despite New Study," LifeNews, August 26, 2010. http://www.lifenews.com/2010/08/26/nat-6659/, last viewed 17 Apr 12.

pregnancy or sexual immorality among their children. We also oppose parental notification when their kids want a government-funded abortion at Planned Parenthood."

<u>Pneumato-Ethics</u>: By objective observation of his ethical choices, we can discern demonic spirits manifesting through Mr. Obama's behavior. *Mr. Obama is ruled, in this instance, by demons of sexual immorality and deception.* The spirits are no longer invisible, but are fully visible, revealed by the ethics they help cause inside the man who promotes sin who promotes sin.

<u>Scripture Mr. Obama Violated</u>: "Flee from sexual immorality. All other sins a man commits are outside his body, but he who sins sexually sins against his own body." 1 Cor. 6:18, NIV.

Event 36. September 2010 – The Obama administration tells researchers to ignore a judge's decision striking down federal funding for embryonic stem cell research.[112]

Desolation: Demonic spirits of tyranny and child-murder (outside, whispering): "Barack, you should ignore the federal judge's pro-life ruling, and violate the law by funding genocide, child-murder, and experimentation that creates and destroys embryos to harvest the babies' body parts to benefit child-murderers."

Consolation: Holy Spirit of life and medical ethics (outside, whispering): "Barack, there are right and wrong ways to conduct medical research, and it is wrong to create and destroy babies for their body parts. Stop the creation and slaughter of innocent children in the laboratory, and stop the genocide against the unborn."

Consent: Barack H. Obama rejects the Holy Spirit and invites the demonic spirit to manifest inside of himself and through his words.

---

[112] Steven Ertelt, "President Barack Obama's Pro-Abortion Record: A Pro-Life Compilation," LifeNews, February 11, 2012. http://www.lifenews.com/2010/11/07/obamaabortionrecord/, last viewed 17 Apr 12.

Manifestation: (Demonic spirit acting through Mr. Obama): "Even after a judge said no, my government will fund the unnecessary creation and destruction of innocent children to be harvested in laboratories for their body parts, to benefit child-murderers."

Pneumato-Ethics: By objective observation of his ethical choices, we can discern demonic spirits manifesting through Mr. Obama's behavior. *Mr. Obama is ruled, in this instance, by demons of tyranny and child-murder.* The spirits are no longer invisible, but are fully visible, revealed by the ethics they help cause inside the man who promotes sin.

Scripture Mr. Obama Violated: "Before I formed you in the womb I knew you, and before you were born I consecrated you; I have appointed you a prophet to the nations." Jeremiah 1:5, NASB.

Event 37. February 2011 – Obama directs the Justice Department to stop defending the federal Defense of Marriage Act.[113]

Desolation: Demonic spirits of tyranny, lawlessness, and sexual immorality (outside, whispering): "Barack, disregard your duty to enforce federal law, especially the 1996 Defense of Marriage Act which defines marriage as only valid between one man and one woman. Promote homosexual immorality by ordering your lawyers to argue for homosexual 'marriage' in courts nationwide."

Consolation: Holy Spirit of purity and faithfulness in marriage (outside, whispering): "Barack, marriage is a symbol of Jesus Christ's covenant with the Church, and is sacred as Jesus defined that in Matthew 19:4-6, between one man and one woman. Defend God's law, and also the 1996 Defense of Marriage Act, to protect God's definition of a traditional family."

Consent: Barack H. Obama rejects the Holy Spirit and invites the demonic spirit to manifest inside of himself and through his words.

---

[113] Brian Montopoli, "Obama administration will no longer defend DOMA," CBSNews, February 23, 2011. http://www.cbsnews.com/8301-503544_162-20035398-503544.html, last viewed 17 Apr 12.

Manifestation: (Demonic spirit acting through Mr. Obama): "I refuse to uphold the law, and neither shall my lawyers obey the law, rather we will impose homosexual 'marriage' upon all 50 states by arguing in courtrooms that sexual immorality has higher moral value than purity."

Pneumato-Ethics: By objective observation of his ethical choices, we can discern demonic spirits manifesting through Mr. Obama's behavior. *Mr. Obama is ruled, in this instance, by demons of lawlessness, tyranny, and sexual immorality.* The spirits are no longer invisible, but are fully visible, revealed by the ethics they help cause inside the man who promotes sin.

Scripture Mr. Obama Violated: "Have you not read that He who created them from the beginning made them male and female, and said, 'for this reason a man shall leave his father and mother and be joined to his wife, and the two shall become one flesh?' So they are no longer two, but one flesh. What therefore God has joined together, let no man separate." Matthew 19:3-6, NASB.

Event 38. March 2011 – The Obama administration refuses to investigate videos showing Planned Parenthood helping alleged sex traffickers get abortions for victimized underage girls.[114]

Desolation: Demonic spirits of child-abuse, sexual abuse, child-murder, injustice (outside, whispering): "Barack, when your political allies in the abortion industry are shown on video promoting child-abuse, sex trafficking, and teenage abortions without parental consent, bury the evidence, don't investigate, and don't prosecute any law-breaking abortionist, ever."

Consolation: Holy Spirit of justice, child-protection, purity, and life (outside, whispering): "Barack, promote justice by protecting children from sex-traffickers, and prosecute and stop abortion providers who facilitate child-abuse, kidnapping, teen prostitution and child-murder of the unborn. If anyone causes one of these little ones who believe in me to sin, it would be better for him to have a large millstone hung around his neck and to be drowned in the

---

[114] Steven Ertelt, "Obama Admin Ignores Planned Parenthood Sex Trafficking Videos," LifeNews, March 2, 2011, http://www.lifenews.com/2011/03/02/obama-admin-ignores-planned-parenthood-sex-trafficking-videos/, last viewed 17 Apr 12.

depths of the sea (Matt 18:6, NIV). Protect children, protect their innocence and purity, and protect life."

Consent: Barack H. Obama rejects the Holy Spirit and invites the demonic spirit to manifest inside of himself and through his words.

Manifestation: (Demonic spirit acting through Mr. Obama): "My administration and Department of 'Injustice' will not investigate or prosecute Planned Parenthood abortion-providers, even if they help sex-trafficking, child-abuse, sexual abuse, or teen abortions without parental consent."

Pneumato-Ethics: By objective observation of his ethical choices, we can discern demonic spirits manifesting through Mr. Obama's behavior. *Mr. Obama is ruled, in this instance, by demons of injustice, child-abuse, sexual abuse, child-murder.*

Scripture Mr. Obama Violated: "'One has committed abomination with his neighbor's wife and another has lewdly defiled his daughter-in-law. And another in you has humbled his sister, his father's daughter. In you they have taken bribes to shed blood; you have taken interest and profits, and you have injured your neighbors for gain by oppression, and you have forgotten Me,' declares the Lord GOD." Ezek. 22:11-12, NASB.

Event 39. July 2011 – Obama allows homosexuals to serve openly in the military, reversing a policy originally instituted by George Washington in March 1778.[115]

Desolation: Demonic spirits of deception, persecution, sexual immorality, sodomy (outside, whispering): "Barack, by deceptively promoting sexual sin as 'equal' to holiness, you can promote sexual perversion and immorality in the name of 'equality,' giving sin a government stamp of approval. Homosexualize the U.S. military, and persecute Christian chaplains who oppose sexual sin, to drive Christians out[116] of the military, and deprive their free speech.[117]"

Consolation: Holy Spirit of truth, purity, and religious freedom (outside, whispering): "Barack, you must protect America, which requires (as our first President Washington

---

[115] Elisabeth Bumiller, "Obama Ends 'Don't Ask, Don't Tell' Policy," New York Times, July 22, 2011, https://www.nytimes.com/2011/07/23/us/23military.html?_r=3, last viewed 17 Apr 12.

[116] "The Real Pentagon Poll: 91% Reject Homosexual Leaders -- 85% of Combat Marines Distrust -- 71% Won't Share Showers -- 24% Won't Re-Enlist," 1 Dec 2010, http://www.christiannewswire.com/news/2297115596.html, last viewed 10 May 2012.

[117] Hope Hodge, "Military religious leaders report pressure, backlash over beliefs," Human Events, 4 May 2012, http://www.humanevents.com/article.php?id=51278, last viewed 10 May 2012.

said) the blessing of God upon our arms. God will not bless our military if they are homosexualized, and Christian troops are persecuted or chaplains are driven out. You must oppose open sodomy and protect religious freedom for military chaplains, especially their free speech right to oppose sin."

Manifestation: (Demonic spirit acting through Mr. Obama): "As commander in chief I will homosexualize our military by deceptively claiming sin is 'equal' to holiness, and I will ensure military chaplains are forced to facilitate homosexual 'weddings' in chapels.[118]"

Pneumato-Ethics: By objective observation of his ethical choices, we can discern demonic spirits manifesting through Mr. Obama's behavior. *Mr. Obama is ruled, in this instance, by demons of deception, persecution, sexual immorality.* The spirits are no longer invisible, but are fully visible, revealed by the ethics they help cause inside the man who promotes sin.

Scripture Mr. Obama Violated: " And there were also sodomites in the land: and they did according to all the abominations of the nations which the LORD cast out before the children of Israel." 1 Kings 14:24, NASB.

---

[118] "Hearing Impaired: DOD tries to Hide Hill Testimony," Family Research Council, http://www.frc.org/washingtonupdate/salvador-dallies-in-gay-rights, last viewed 10 May 12.

Event 40. September 2011 – The Pentagon directs that military chaplains [must facilitate and] may perform same-sex marriages at military facilities in violation of the federal Defense of Marriage Act [DOMA].[119]

Desolation: Demonic spirits of lawlessness, sexual immorality, persecution and desecration (outside, whispering): "Barack, not only should you force military chaplains to facilitate homosexual 'marriages' in all 50 states, you should threaten those who refuse to turn over the keys to their Christian or Catholic chapel building for sodomite desecration. Deny all troops their right to protect a sacred worship space at the Christian altar."

Consolation: Holy Spirit of religious freedom (outside, whispering): "Barack, you must protect military chaplains and troops sacred right to worship at a sacred place, especially the Christian or Catholic altar consecrated in every military chapel, which must never be desecrated by sodomy."

---

[119] Luis Martinez, "Will Same Sex Marriages Pose a Dilemma for Military Chaplains?," ABC News, October 12, 2011. http://abcnews.go.com/blogs/politics/2011/10/will-same-sex-marriages-pose-a-dilemma-for-military-chaplains/, last viewed 17 Apr 12.

Consent: Barack H. Obama rejects the Holy Spirit and invites the demonic spirit to manifest inside of himself and through his words.

Manifestation: (Demonic spirit acting through Mr. Obama): "My Pentagon lawyer Jeh Johnson will write a memo authorizing homosexual weddings in all military chapels in all 50 states, desecrating the sacred worship space of Christians and Catholics, and violating DOMA law."

Pneumato-Ethics: By objective observation of his ethical choices, we can discern demonic spirits manifesting through Mr. Obama's behavior. *Mr. Obama is ruled, in this instance, by demons of lawlessness, sexual immorality, persecution, and desecration.* The spirits are no longer invisible, but are fully visible, revealed by the ethics they help cause inside the man who promotes sin.

Scripture Mr. Obama Violated: "You shall not lie with a man, as with a woman: it is abomination." Leviticus 18:22, KJV.

Event 41. October 2011 – The Obama administration eliminates federal grants to the U.S. Conference of Catholic Bishops for their extensive programs that aid victims of human trafficking because the Catholic Church is anti-abortion.[120]

Desolation: Demonic spirits of anti-Christian persecution (outside, whispering): "Barack, make sure your staff eliminates any government funding for the poor, if those poor happen to be served by Christian ministries. Discriminate against pro-lifers and only pay tax-dollars to abortionists."

Consolation: Holy Spirit of justice, life, faith (outside, whispering): "Barack, do not punish or exclude Christians simply because they refuse to kill children. If anything you should stop funding child-murderers, and send tax dollars to charities who care for the poor without killing their children."

Consent: Barack H. Obama rejects the Holy Spirit and invites the demonic spirit to manifest inside of himself and through his words.

---

[120] Jerry Markon, "Health, abortion issues split Obama administration and Catholic groups," Washington Post, October 31, 2011. http://www.washingtonpost.com/politics/health-abortion-issues-split-obama-administration-catholic-groups/2011/10/27/gIQAXV5xZM_story.html, last viewed 17 Apr 12.

Manifestation: (Demonic spirit acting through Mr. Obama): "My administration will eliminate federal grants for any charities that serve the poor if those charity leaders have pro-life beliefs."

Pneumato-Ethics: By objective observation of his ethical choices, we can discern demonic spirits manifesting through Mr. Obama's behavior. *Mr. Obama is ruled, in this instance, by demons of child-murder and anti-Christian persecution.* The spirits are no longer invisible, but are fully visible, revealed by the ethics they help cause inside the man who promotes sin.

Scripture Mr. Obama Violated: "A person who gets ahead by oppressing the poor or by showering gifts on the rich will end in poverty." Proverbs 22:16, NLT

Event 42. May 2009 – While Obama does not host any National Day of Prayer event at the White House, he does host White House Iftar [Muslim] dinners in honor of Ramadan.[121]

Desolation: Demonic spirits of idolatry, false worship (outside, whispering): "Barack, you must refuse to affiliate with ministers of the Judeo-Christian tradition, and never host a ceremony for the National Day of Prayer. Instead show outlandish favor to Muslim holidays, Imams, and pray publicly to the false god Allah of the false religion Islam to honor the false prophet Mohammed."

Consolation: Holy Spirit of true worship of the One God of Abraham, Isaac, Jacob, and Jesus (outside, whispering): "Barack, I am the LORD your God, you shall have no other gods before me. I the LORD am One God, the father of Abraham, Isaac, Jacob, and I became flesh in the

---

[121] Alexander Mooney, "President Obama marks Ramadan," CNN, August 1, 2011. http://www.whitehouse.gov/the_press_office/Remarks-by-the-President-at-Iftar-Dinner/, last viewed 17 Apr 12; Kristi Keck, "Obama tones down National Day of Prayer observance," *CNN*, May 6, 2009, http://articles.cnn.com/2009-05-06/politics/obama.prayer_1_national-day-prayer-observance-prayer-task-force?_s=PM:POLITICS, last viewed 17 Apr 12; Dan Gilgoff, " The White House on National Day of Prayer: A Proclamation, but No Formal Ceremony," *U.S. News*, May 1, 2009, http://www.usnews.com/news/blogs/god-and-country/2009/05/01/the-white-house-on-national-day-of-prayer-a-proclamation-but-no-formal-ceremony, last viewed 17 Apr 12.

person of my son Jesus Christ. You must worship me alone, and never worship idols."

Consent: Barack H. Obama rejects the Holy Spirit and invites the demonic spirit to manifest inside of himself and through his words.

Manifestation: (Demonic spirit acting through Mr. Obama): "I will reject the Judeo-Christian God and I will refuse to participate in the National Day of Prayer, but instead I will repeatedly celebrate Muslim Ramadan, and host Islamic dinners, prayers, and Imams to worship Allah."

Pneumato-Ethics: By objective observation of his ethical choices, we can discern demonic spirits manifesting through Mr. Obama's behavior. *Mr. Obama is ruled, in this instance, by demons of idolatry and false worship.* The spirits are no longer invisible, but are fully visible, revealed by the ethics they help cause inside the man who promotes sin.

Scripture Mr. Obama Violated: "Jesus said to him, "I am the way, and the truth, and the life; no one comes to the Father but through Me." John 14:6, NASB.

Event 43. April 2010 – Christian leader Franklin Graham is dis-invited from the Pentagon's National Day of Prayer Event because of complaints from the Muslim community.[122]

Desolation: Demonic spirits of persecution, anti-Christian censorship (outside, whispering): "Barack, make sure your staff specifically fires or disinvites Christian speakers like Franklin Graham because he prays in Jesus' name and because he quotes the scriptures against false religions like Islam. In false inclusivity, the Pentagon must exclude evangelical Christianity."

Consolation: Holy Spirit of truth and religious freedom (outside, whispering): "Barack, celebrate the Judeo-Christian tradition of the National Day of Prayer, or at least allow your military leaders and chaplains to invite evangelical speakers who proclaim the Truth of God's Word and speak boldly for truth and religious freedom."

---

[122] "Franklin Graham Regrets Army's Decision to Rescind Invite to Pentagon Prayer Service," Fox News, April 22, 2010.
http://www.foxnews.com/politics/2010/04/21/army-weighs-rescinding-invitation-evangelist/, last viewed 17 Apr 12.

Consent: Barack H. Obama rejects the Holy Spirit and invites the demonic spirit to manifest inside of himself and through his words.

Manifestation: (Demonic spirit acting through Mr. Obama): "My Pentagon staffers must not allow Franklin Graham or evangelical Christians or chaplains to speak publicly about Jesus Christ, nor tell troops how they can pray in Jesus' name, nor how they can gain eternal salvation through Jesus Christ, even at optionally attended events like the National Day of Prayer."

Pneumato-Ethics: By objective observation of his ethical choices, we can discern demonic spirits manifesting through Mr. Obama's behavior. *Mr. Obama is ruled, in this instance, by demons of anti-Christian censorship and persecution.* The spirits are no longer invisible, but are fully visible, revealed by the ethics they help cause inside the man who promotes sin.

Scripture Mr. Obama Violated: "If you suffer as a Christian, do not be ashamed, but praise God that you bear that name." 1 Peter 4:16, NASB.

http://ObamasDemons.com

Event 44. April 2010 – The Obama administration requires rewriting of government documents and a change in administration vocabulary to remove terms that are deemed offensive to Muslims, including jihad, jihadists, terrorists, radical Islamic, etc.[123]

Desolation: Demonic spirits of lying, idolatry, totalitarian oppression (outside, whispering): "Barack, order your staff to revise history in favor of Islam, by going through all government documents to change the meaning of terrorism and jihad. Pretend those who hate America are not motivated by their religious beliefs in the violent teachings of Islam or their false prophet."

Consolation: Holy Spirit of truth and historical accuracy (outside, whispering): "Barack, don't confuse people, especially military planners, about the true enemy of freedom, religious totalitarianism, which teaches the false

---

[123] "Obama Bans Islam, Jihad From National Security Strategy Document," Fox News, April 7, 2010, http://www.foxnews.com/politics/2010/04/07/obama-bans-islam-jihad-national-security-strategy-document/, last viewed 17 Apr 12; "Counterterror Adviser Defends Jihad as 'Legitimate Tenet of Islam'," Fox News, May 27, 2010, http://www.foxnews.com/politics/2010/05/27/counterterror-adviser-defends-jihad-legitimate-tenet-islam/, last viewed 17 Apr 12; "'Islamic Radicalism' Nixed From Obama Document," CBS News, April 7, 2010, http://www.cbsnews.com/stories/2010/04/07/politics/main6371159.shtml, last viewed 17 Apr 12.

religion of Islam as a systematic governmental oppression that intends and teaches violence toward all who oppose it. Mohammed conquers with the sword, and our Christian citizens have a right to defend themselves against evil."

Consent: Barack H. Obama rejects the Holy Spirit and invites the demonic spirit to manifest inside of himself and through his words.

Manifestation: (Demonic spirit acting through Mr. Obama): "My government will sympathize with Muslim terrorists, and we will intentionally fail to describe the jihad of violence against Christians and Jews taught by Mohammed as if it is the enemy of religious freedom."

Pneumato-Ethics: By objective observation of his ethical choices, we can discern demonic spirits manifesting through Mr. Obama's behavior. *Mr. Obama is ruled, in this instance, by demons of lying, idolatry, and totalitarian oppression.* The spirits are no longer invisible, but are fully visible, revealed by the ethics they help cause inside the man who promotes sin.

Scripture Mr. Obama Violated: "Joyful are people of integrity, who follow the instructions of the LORD…They do not compromise with evil, and they walk only in his paths." Psalm 119:1-3, NASB.

Event 45. August 2010 – Obama speaks with great praise of Islam and condescendingly of Christianity.[124]

Desolation: Demonic spirits of idolatry, mockery, hatred of Christ (outside): "Barack, you are a son of Islam, as your father before you, and you must not only worship the false god Allah, but also mock and belittle Jesus Christ or Christians who worship the True God."

Consolation: Holy Spirit of truth and faithfulness to the True God through Jesus Christ (outside, whispering): "Barack, heed the words of Jesus Christ, who said in John 14:6, 'I am the way, the truth, and the life, no man comes to the Father except through me."

Consent: Barack H. Obama rejects the Holy Spirit and invites the demonic spirit to manifest inside of himself and through his words.

Manifestation: (Demonic spirit acting through Mr. Obama's specific speech): "I lived in Indonesia, the largest Muslim country in the world. ... I believe that there are many paths to the same place. ... I retain from my childhood and

---

[124] Chuck Norris, "President Obama: Muslim Missionary?," Townhall.com, August 17, 2010, http://townhall.com/columnists/chucknorris/2010/08/24/obama_muslim_missionary_part_2/page/full/, last viewed 17 Apr 12.

my experiences growing up a suspicion of dogma. ... There's an enormous amount of damage done around the world in the name of religion and certainty. ... I find it hard to believe that my God would consign four-fifths of the world to hell. ... That's just not part of my religious makeup…Whatever we once were, we are no longer a Christian nation; the dangers of sectarianism are greater than ever."[125]

<u>Pneumato-Ethics</u>: By objective observation of his ethical choices, we can discern demonic spirits manifesting through Mr. Obama's behavior. *Mr. Obama is ruled, in this instance, by demons of idolatry, mockery, and rejection of Christ.* The spirits are no longer invisible, but are fully visible, revealed by the ethics they help cause inside the man who promotes sin.

<u>Scripture Mr. Obama Violated</u>: "By the name of Jesus Christ of Nazareth, whom ye crucified, whom God raised from the dead…Neither is there salvation in any other: for there is none other name under heaven given among men, whereby we must be saved." Acts 4:10-12, NASB.

---

[125] Ibid.

Event 46. August 2010 – Obama went to great lengths to speak out on multiple occasions on behalf of building an Islamic mosque at Ground Zero, while at the same time he was silent about a Christian church being denied permission to rebuild at that location.[126]

Desolation: Demonic spirits of idolatry and promotion of false gods (outside, whispering): "Barack, you should promote Islam as a religion deserving freedom, not as a politically totalitarian ideology that oppresses the freedoms of others, and advocates killing dissenters by sword. Never mention Islam's goal to conquer America by violent slaughter at Ground Zero."

Consolation: Holy Spirit of respect for the victims of 9/11 (outside, whispering): "Barack, don't allow the enemies of religious freedom to declare victory over the victims of Islamic terror. Honor religious freedom for the victims of 9/11 by allowing a church, not the terrorists' mosque."

---

[126] "Obama Comes Out in Favor of Allowing Mosque Near Ground Zero," Fox News, August 13, 2010, http://www.foxnews.com/politics/2010/08/13/obama-backs-mosque-near-ground-zero/, last viewed 17 Apr 12; Pamela Geller, "Islamic Supremacism Trumps Christianity at Ground Zero," American Thinker, July 21, 2011. http://www.americanthinker.com/2011/07/islamic_supremacism_trumps_christianity_at_ground_zero.html, last viewed 17 Apr 12.

<u>Consent</u>: Barack H. Obama rejects the Holy Spirit and invites the demonic spirit to manifest inside of himself and through his words.

<u>Manifestation</u>: (Demonic spirit acting through Mr. Obama): "We must honor the terrorists, not the victims, by defending their right to build an Islamic Mosque on the site of Ground Zero."

<u>Pneumato-Ethics</u>: By objective observation of his ethical choices, we can discern demonic spirits manifesting through Mr. Obama's behavior. *Mr. Obama is ruled, in this instance, by demons of idolatry and hatred of religious freedom, honoring the 'religion' of those who kill Christians.* The spirits are no longer invisible, but are fully visible, revealed by the ethics they help cause inside the man who promotes sin.

<u>Scripture Mr. Obama Violated</u>: "Do not set up any wooden Asherah pole beside the altar you build to the LORD your God," Deuteronomy 16:21, NASB.

"If the land you possess is defiled, come over to the LORD's land, where the LORD's tabernacle stands, and share the land with us. But do not rebel against the LORD or against us by building an altar for yourselves, other than the altar of the LORD our God." Joshua 22:19, NIV.

Event 47. 2010 – While every White House traditionally issues hundreds of official proclamations and statements on numerous occasions, this White House avoids traditional Biblical holidays and events [such as Easter] but regularly recognizes major Muslim holidays, as evidenced by its 2010 statements on Ramadan, Eid-ul-Fitr, Hajj, and Eid-ul-Adha.[127]

Desolation: Demonic spirits who hate and avoid all things Christian (outside, whispering): "Barack, it would be insensitive to non-Christians if you ever mention Easter, but you must be sensitive to Muslims by repeatedly honoring all of their holidays ad nauseum with great fanfare."

Consolation: Holy Spirit of truth (outside, whispering): "Barack, the truth is Jesus Christ rose from the dead for the forgiveness of all sins for all people who accept Jesus Christ as Lord and Savior. If any holiday deserves

---

[127] "WH Fails to Release Easter Proclamation," Fox Nation, April 25, 2011, http://nation.foxnews.com/president-obama/2011/04/25/wh-fails-release-easter-proclamation, last viewed 17 Apr 12; "President Obama ignores most holy Christian holiday; AFA calls act intentional," American Family Association (accessed on February 29, 2012), http://www.afa.net/Detail.aspx?id=2147505615, last viewed 17 Apr 12. Note that after much public criticism directed at the White House spokesman, Mr. Obama finally, reluctantly issued an Easter proclamation in 2012.

public proclamation, it is Resurrection Day, for Christ is risen."

<u>Consent</u>: Barack H. Obama rejects the Holy Spirit and invites the demonic spirit to manifest inside of himself and through his words.

<u>Manifestation</u>: (Demonic spirit acting through Mr. Obama): "I will issue public proclamations for every possible Muslim holiday, to honor Muslims, but I will avoid mention of Christian holidays, so that I don't offend non-Christians with words like 'Jesus' or 'Easter' or 'resurrection.'"

<u>Pneumato-Ethics</u>: By objective observation of his ethical choices, we can discern demonic spirits manifesting through Mr. Obama's behavior. *Mr. Obama is ruled, in this instance, by demons of cowardice and ashamedness of Jesus Christ.* The spirits are no longer invisible, but are fully visible, revealed by the ethics they help cause inside the man who promotes sin.

<u>Scripture Mr. Obama Violated</u>: "You must not worship the LORD your God in their way, because in worshiping their gods, they do all kinds of detestable things the LORD hates." Deuteronomy 12:31, NIV.

Event 48. October 2011 – Obama's Muslim advisers block Middle Eastern Christians' access to the White House.[128]

Desolation: Demonic spirits of exclusion and punishment of Christians (outside, whispering): "Barack, surround yourself with staffers who intentionally exclude Christians from participating in policy discussions inside the White House, and instead give policy favor and access to atheist, Muslim, or homosexual groups."

Consolation: Holy Spirit of (outside, whispering): "Barack, discipline your staff to never discriminate against Christians or people who love the True God, the Father of Jesus Christ. In fact you should welcome their input, because it is ultimately informed by the Holy Spirit."

Consent: Barack H. Obama rejects the Holy Spirit and invites the demonic spirit to manifest inside of himself and through his words.

Manifestation: (Demonic spirit acting through Mr. Obama): "My staffers should specifically favor Islam and

---

[128] "Report: Obama's Muslim Advisers Block Middle Eastern Christians' Access to the White House," Atlas Shrugged, 27 Oct 11, http://atlasshrugs2000.typepad.com/atlas_shrugs/2011/10/obamas-muslim-advisers-block-middle-eastern-christians-access-to-white-house.html, last viewed 17 Apr 12.

exclude Christians from access to policy discussions at the White House."

Pneumato-Ethics: By objective observation of his ethical choices, we can discern demonic spirits manifesting through Mr. Obama's behavior. *Mr. Obama is ruled, in this instance, by demons of anti-Christian exclusion and persecution.* The spirits are no longer invisible, but are fully visible, revealed by the ethics they help cause inside the man who promotes sin.

Scripture Mr. Obama Violated:

"Woe to those who make unjust laws,

to those who issue oppressive decrees,

to deprive the poor of their rights

and withhold justice from the oppressed of my people,

making widows their prey

and robbing the fatherless."

Isaiah 10:1-2, NIV.

Event 49. February 2012 – The Obama administration makes effulgent apologies for Korans being burned by the United States military.[129]

Desolation: Demonic spirits of promotion of Islam over freedom of the press (outside, whispering): "Barack, when our troops perform their mission by shredding or burning classified intelligence data including terrorist communication notes written by Afghan prisoners in their prisoner copies of the Koran, you should punish our American troops for offending Islam."

Consolation: Holy Spirit of sanity and freedom of the press (outside, whispering): "Barack, religious freedom of the press also includes freedom to oppose idolatrous ideas in some books, which directly and indirectly promote terrorism, and may be destroyed by our troops in the interest of freedom, which trumps your unconstitutional favoritism of one heretical sect's book."

---

[129] Masoud Popalzai and Nick Paton Walsh, "Obama apologizes to Afghanistan for Quran burning," *CNN*, February 23, 2012, http://www.cnn.com/2012/02/23/world/asia/afghanistan-burned-qurans/index.html?hpt=hp_t1, last viewed 17 Apr 12; "USA/Afghanistan-Islamophobia: Pentagon official apologizes for Quran burning," International Islamic News Agency, http://iina.me/wp_en/?p=1006994, last viewed 17 Apr 12.

Consent: Barack H. Obama rejects the Holy Spirit and invites the demonic spirit to manifest inside of himself and through his words.

Manifestation: (Demonic spirit acting through Mr. Obama): "I will not only apologize for our troops inadvertent burning of some Muslim books, I will initiate a witch-hunt to investigate, find, and punish our troops for their 'crime' of offending Islam."

Pneumato-Ethics: By objective observation of his ethical choices, we can discern demonic spirits manifesting through Mr. Obama's behavior. *Mr. Obama is ruled, in this instance, by demons of idolatry, oppression, and hatred of religious freedom and freedom of the press.* The spirits are no longer invisible, but are fully visible, revealed by the ethics they help cause inside the man who promotes sin.

Scripture Mr. Obama Violated: "Many of the believers began to confess openly and tell all the evil things they had done. Some of them who had used magic brought their magic books and burned them before everyone. Those books were worth about fifty thousand silver coins. So in a powerful way the word of the Lord kept spreading and growing." Acts 19:18-20.

Event 50. April 2009 -- when Bibles were burned by the military, numerous reasons were offered why it was the 'right' thing to do.[130]

Desolation: Demonic spirits of hatred of Christian teachings and hatred of the Bible (outside, whispering): "Barack, when Christian churches in America volunteer to buy and ship Bibles to support our troops in Afghanistan, make sure to seize and burn the Bibles as illegal contraband, then defend the policy of burning the Bibles because you must never offend non-Christians."

Consolation: Holy Spirit of Biblical Truth and Religious Freedom of the Press (outside, whispering): "Barack, true religious freedom means Christians must be allowed to print and distribute their own books, especially during optional Christian worship meetings in church. Give our troops the same religious freedom of the press they defend for others, and deserve for themselves. Don't seize and burn our troops' privately funded Bibles."

---

[130] "Military burns unsolicited Bibles sent to Afghanistan," CNN, May 22, 2009, http://edition.cnn.com/2009/WORLD/asiapcf/05/20/us.military.bibles.burned/, last viewed 17 Apr 12.

Consent: Barack H. Obama rejects the Holy Spirit and invites the demonic spirit to manifest inside of himself and through his words.

Manifestation: (Demonic spirit acting through Mr. Obama): "Our government must never offend violent Muslims in Afghanistan, therefore our troops' privately-owned Bibles should be seized and burned by unethical military leaders who hate freedom of the press."

Pneumato-Ethics: By objective observation of his ethical choices, we can discern demonic spirits manifesting through Mr. Obama's behavior. *Mr. Obama is ruled, in this instance, by demons of fear of offending Muslims, theft, destruction, censorship, and persecution of Christians.* The spirits are no longer invisible, but are fully visible, revealed by the ethics they help cause inside the man who promotes sin.

Scripture Mr. Obama Violated: "From infancy you have known the holy Scriptures, which are able to make you wise for salvation through faith in Christ Jesus. All Scripture is God-breathed and is useful for teaching, rebuking, correcting and training in righteousness." 2 Tim 3:15-16, NIV.

In conclusion of this chapter, we have identified the following groups of demonic spirits that routinely manifest in the soul of the 44th President of the United States, Barack H. Obama:

Demons of Death, Murder, Child-Murder, and Genocide.

Demons of Sexual Immorality and Child-Perversion.

Demons of Tyranny, Lawlessness and Injustice.

Demons of Deception and False Accusation.

Demons of Homosexual Lust and the promotion thereof.

Demons of Child-Abuse and Sexual Abuse.

Demons of Lying, Mockery, and Rejection or Ashamedness of Christ.

Demons of Cowardice and Fear of Offending Muslims.

Demons of Censorship, Theft, or Destruction of all things Christian.

Demons of anti-Christian Persecution, Exclusion, Desecration, Oppression.

Demons of Idolatry and False Worship of Islam.

Demons of Hatred of Religious Freedom and Freedom of the Press.

By his own free will cooperation with these demonic spirits, whose identities are revealed by their immoral character, Mr. Obama has allowed these specific demons to rule his own will, by his own voluntary consent. Because he chooses these sins voluntarily, Mr. Obama is fully responsible, and was not forced to do evil. Yet because he fully cooperates with the demonic beings that whisper their immoral suggestions to his mind, Mr. Obama consents to allow these demons full access, entrance, and manifestation through his body to display their own evil personalities. The demons are no longer invisible, but can be plainly seen, if you have spiritual eyes, since the non-human spirits are revealed by the immoral actions and policies of the man. We have also discerned the Holy Spirit, and His likely alternative suggestions as whispered to Mr. Obama's conscience, but since he routinely ignores the Holy Spirit, and hardens his own heart and conscience against the Spirit of God, Mr. Obama voluntarily refuses to allow the Spirit of God access, entry, or manifestation through his body. We cannot see the Holy Spirit manifesting through Mr. Obama, instead we see the Holy Spirit grieved and rejected, as Christ and Christians have been by political leaders throughout time.

In the final pages next I will offer some overall observations and conclusions, first about the spiritual gift of discerning of spirits, then about the demons (revealed by his policies and actions) ruling the soul of Barack H. Obama.

http://ObamasDemons.com

GET TEN FREE COPIES OF THIS E-BOOK, NOW.

This e-book is available on AMAZON.COM for $2.95 U.S. and other outlets including CreateSpace.com and ObamasDemons.com.

This e-book & PDF are copyrighted, and may not be emailed.

However, if you purchased this e-book and email to us your e-receipt, you may obtain a FREE license to distribute the entire PDF of this e-book (as is), to up to 10 friends by email, so this e-book will be FREE for your 10 friends. Register now and email your receipt to license@obamasdemons.com. We will automatically email you a free distributor's license.

(FYI, the paperback for $9.95 is not part of this offer.)

GOT A LARGER EMAIL LIST?

You may also purchase a larger license to email this e-book more widely, to more than ten friends, at these rates:

License to email this e-book to:	Cost:
20 extra friends at 50 cents each	$ 9.95
50 extra friends at 40 cents each	$ 19.95
100 extra friends at 30 cents each	$ 29.95
200 friends at 20 cents each	$ 39.95
300 friends at 17 cents each	$ 49.95
500 friends at 14 cents each	$ 69.95
1000 friends at 10 cents each	$ 99.95

Over 1000 friends: $ 99.95 plus .05 per friend over 1000.

VISIT http://ObamasDemons.com TO BUY A LICENSE.

Conclusion: The Demons Ruling Barack H. Obama

If you opened this book hoping to find a specific list of Demons that rule the 44th President of the United States, I hope I have fulfilled your curiosity.

Maybe you think by now, "Well, Mr. Obama claims to be a Christian, so maybe he's just got a few sin issues. Maybe he's not really ruled by demonic beings or the devil." But again, I direct you to please consider 1 John 3:8-10: "The one who practices sin is of the devil; for the devil has sinned from the beginning. The Son of God appeared for this purpose, to destroy the works of the devil. No one who is born of God practices sin, because His seed abides in him; and he cannot sin, because he is born of God. By this the children of God and the children of the devil are obvious: anyone who does not practice righteousness is not of God, nor the one who does not love his brother." (NASB).

You cannot fully embrace this scripture's meaning, unless you conclude that sin is always demonic, period. The one who practices sin, is of the devil, or ruled by demons.

It is wiser in my estimation, to discern the spirits inside the man, than pretend they're not really there. With this in mind, here is the completed list, as previously discovered by objective pneumato-ethical analysis of 50 historical events.

Mr. Obama's heart is ruled by:

Demons of Persecution of the Church.

Demons of Tyranny, Secularization and Censorship.

Demons of Anti-Christian Oppression and Hostility.

Demons of Witchcraft, Paganism and Idolatry.

Demons that Forbid or Punish Acts of Christian Charity.

Demons that Threaten or Ban Bible Readers.

Demons that Oppress or Silence Christian Leaders.

Demons bent on Destruction of the Church.

Demons that promote Sexual Immorality.

Demons that openly Mock Religion and People of Faith.

Demons of Defiant Rebellion against Love and Purity.

Demons of Ingratitude toward God.

Demons Ashamed of God, Refusing to Honor, Memorialize, or Acknowledge God.

Demons of Historical Revision who Deny God as Creator.

Demons of Death and Disrespect for Human Life.

Demons who Neglect/publicly Reject expressions of Prayer.

Demons Ashamed of Christ, who oppose or forbid the public display of the Cross.

Demons of Lying and Historical Revisionism.

Demons pressuring Christians to Violate their Conscience and Disobey God.

Demons of Mockery, Disdain, and Belittling of Christians' Religious Beliefs.

Demons of Death, Murder, Child-murder, and Genocide.

Demons of Sexual Immorality and Child-Perversion.

Demons of Tyranny, Lawlessness and Injustice.

Demons of Deception and False Accusation.

Demons of Homosexual Lust and the promotion thereof.

Demons of Child-Abuse and Sexual Abuse.

Demons of Lying, Mockery, and Rejection or Ashamedness of Christ.

Demons of Cowardice and Fear of Offending Muslims.

Demons of Censorship, Theft, or Destruction of all things Christian.

Demons of anti-Christian Persecution, Exclusion, Desecration, Oppression.

Demons of Idolatry and False Worship of Islam.

Demons of Hatred of Religious Freedom and Freedom of the Press.

In general, these groups of demons may be organized into four main categories:

1) Demons that promote Sexual Immorality.
2) Demons that promote Murder of Innocent Children.
3) Demons that promote False Religions.
4) Demons that Persecute the Christian church.

There can be no doubt, theologically, that each of these four categories of behaviors is described in the Bible as sin. I have thoroughly discussed the scriptures relating sin to the Gift of Discerning of Spirits in Chapter 1.

There can be no doubt, spiritually, that each of these four categories of sins is also demonic. I have thoroughly discussed the Rules for Discerning of Spirits in Chapter 2.

There can be no doubt, pneumato-ethically, that Mr. Obama is manifesting demonic spirits, and voluntarily allowing them to rule his heart, mind, will, and choices, in each of the 50 events described in Chapters 3 and 4.

In this way I have demonstrated, by objective analysis of historical events using a systematic Biblical and Ignatian method, that Mr. Obama voluntarily cooperates with demons whom he invites to rule and indwell his heart, mind, soul, and will, so their non-human, evil immorality manifests inside and through his human character.

I therefore broadly conclude that Mr. Obama is ruled by demons who promote the sins of murder, sexual immorality, idolatry, and tyranny against the Church.

This book neither endorses nor opposes Mr. Obama's candidacy for any office. You are free to vote for whomever you choose. Please do, however, when making your choices and evaluating this man (or any human), look a little deeper into his soul. Is the Holy Spirit of Jesus Christ ruling his heart and causing voluntary holiness, or are demonic spirits ruling his heart and inspiring sin and evil moral character?

More importantly, and myself included, we should all self-examine our own hearts and morality. Again I invite all readers to pray with me this simple prayer of humility, for greater discernment of the spirits around us:

A HUMBLE PRAYER FOR DISCERNMENT:

"God I repent for my own sins first. God help me remove the log from my own eye first, right now, today. Then when my own heart is clean, please equip me to see more accurately into the hearts of others, not so I may judge them, but so I may help them know God. Let the church be holy first, before we attempt to clean up the political culture. Lord Jesus Christ, rule my heart today, and fill me with your Holy Spirit, as I willfully consent to allow God's true moral character to indwell me, and manifest Your holiness through my words and deeds. I renounce all my known sins and demons. Get them out of me, so I can see clearly to minister the forgiveness of Christ to others, and begin to exorcise and cast out the demons in the world around me. In Jesus' name, Amen."

Is He the Anti-Christ?

Afterword by Pastor Ernie Sanders

We may never fully recognize the true identity of the coming Anti-Christ. But is it a coincidence, or not, that so many Bible references to the Anti-Christ also refer, at least indirectly, to Barack H. Obama?

In Luke 10:18, KJV Jesus said, "I beheld Satan as lightning fall from heaven." The word for lightning is "baraq" in Hebrew בָּרָק. In the Aramaic Jesus spoke it's "beraq;" transliterated to English lightning means Barack.

Isaiah 14:12-14 says "How art thou fallen from heaven, O Lucifer, son of the morning!...For thou hast said in thine heart, I will ascend into heaven, I will exalt my throne above the stars of God... I will ascend above the heights of the clouds; I will be like the most High." The Hebrew words for "heights of the clouds" is מָתֵי בָּבַע transliterated 'āb bā·mo·tê or Obama.

When this Hebrew word for "heights of the clouds" is often translated as "heaven" then both words, Barack Obama, are easily seen in Luke 10:18, where Jesus saw Satan falling as Barack (lightning) from Obama (high place or heaven).

Ezekiel 20:29 confirms this translation, saying: "What is the high place whereunto ye go? And the name thereof is called

Bamah unto this day….Are ye polluted after the manner of your fathers? and commit ye whoredom after their abominations?" So the land O'bama is described in the Bible as a place of many abominations.

Ezekiel 22 explains those abominations, which resemble the bloody pro-abortion and idolatrous pro-Islam policies of the Obama Administration: "Thou shalt shew her all her abominations. Then say thou, Thus saith the Lord GOD, The city sheddeth blood in the midst of it, that her time may come, and maketh idols against herself to defile herself. Thou art become guilty in thy blood that thou hast shed; and hast defiled thyself in thine idols which thou hast made."

Matthew 24:15 refers to the Anti-Christ, warning "When ye therefore shall see the abomination of desolation, spoken of by Daniel the prophet, stand in the holy place, (whoso readeth, let him understand)." Does not Mr. Obama cause desolation and abomination?

Daniel 7:20, 25 describes the Anti-Christ, saying "even of that horn that had eyes, and a mouth that spake very great things, whose look was more stout [pompous or smug] than his fellows. I beheld, and the same horn made war with the saints, and prevailed against them…And he shall speak great words against the most High, and shall wear out the saints of the most High, and think to change times and laws." By openly persecuting the Church in many ways, promoting homosexual 'marriage,' and changing military sodomy from a federal crime to a prideful celebration, Obama has changed the times and laws, and he wears out the saints. He fits nearly every Biblical criteria.

2 Thessalonians 2:8 refers to the Anti-Christ as "that **lawless one** will be revealed whom the Lord will slay with the breath of His mouth and bring to an end by His coming." Why is Mr. Obama's secret service nickname "Renegade" which term the dictionary defines as a "lawless one" or "an apostate from a religious faith?"

Revelation 13:18 says "Here is wisdom. Let him that hath understanding count the number of the beast: for it is the number of a man; and his number is Six hundred threescore and six." Not surprisingly, the secret service refers to Mr. Obama's armor-plated limousine as "The Beast." When he served as State Senator in Illinois, the zip code for Obama's office was 60606. And on the day Mr. Obama won the Democrat nomination to become President, guess what the winning pick-three Illinois lottery numbers were? 666.

These facts are no coincidence. They point to a man of sin. If Mr. Obama is not The Anti-Christ, he is certainly ruled by anti-Christian demons. I heartily endorse Chaplain Klingenschmitt's book, The Demons of Barack H. Obama.

--Pastor Ernie Sanders, Novelty Ohio
Doers of The Word Baptist Church (wrwl.org)

http://ObamasDemons.com

Stay tuned for the planned sequel, forthcoming in 2013:

The Demons of Willard "Mitt" Romney

ABOUT THE AUTHOR: WHO IS GJK?

Chaplain Gordon James Klingenschmitt, Ph.D., D.D. is the founder and servant of The Pray in Jesus Name Project, leading a network that reaches 80,000 U.S. pastors annually and 30,000 subscribers daily who helped him deliver over 4 Million fax petitions to the U.S. Congress, defending pro-life, pro-marriage, pro-Israel and pro-Jesus liberties.

As a former U.S. Navy Chaplain, he was instrumental in standing up for the rights of military chaplains to pray publicly "in Jesus' name." In 2006 he was vindicated by the U.S. Congress, who rescinded the bad prayer policy which had wrongly inhibited his free speech.

Dr. Klingenschmitt has served as a Bible teacher for the past twenty-one years, on 200+ radio shows, in 100+ churches, college campuses and military bases in 27 states and overseas. He is a certified Master Instructor and Academic Instructor School graduate, having taught Quality Air Force management courses for five years.

Dr. Klingenschmitt also served as an Air Force missile officer, intelligence officer, and management consultant advising numerous commanding generals over 45,000 employees. An expert marksman with a parachutist badge, he volunteered for a demotion and a pay cut to become Navy Chaplain, and was honorably discharged. He has advised or served six U.S. Presidential Candidates.

Dr. Klingenschmitt is an award-winning published author of several academic works, including *Discerning the Spirits in Ecclesial Ethics: Ignatius of Loyola and the Pneumatological Foundations of Ecclesiology*. He has been interviewed on the Christian Broadcasting Network, Hannity & Colmes, PBS, NPR, Fox News, CNN, MSNBC and Trinity Broadcasting Network.

Dr. Klingenschmitt earned his Bachelor of Science degree in political science from the United States Air Force Academy, a Master of Business Administration, Master of Divinity and Doctor of Philosophy degrees from Regent University. He also received an honorary Doctor of Divinity degree from Military Bible Association.

Dr. Klingenschmitt resides in Colorado Springs, Colorado with his wife of 21 years, Mary, and may be contacted via prayinjesusname.org.

http://ObamasDemons.com

GET TEN FREE COPIES OF THIS E-BOOK, NOW.

This e-book is available on AMAZON.COM for $2.95 U.S. and other outlets including CreateSpace.com and ObamasDemons.com. This e-book & PDF are copyrighted, and may not be emailed.

However, if you purchased this e-book and email to us your e-receipt, you may obtain a FREE license to distribute the entire PDF of this e-book (as is), to up to 10 friends by email, so this e-book will be FREE for your 10 friends. Register now and email your receipt to license@obamasdemons.com. We will automatically email you a free distributor's license. (FYI, the paperback for $9.95 is not part of this offer.)

GOT A LARGER EMAIL LIST?

You may also purchase a larger license to email this e-book more widely, to more than ten friends, at these rates:

License to email this e-book to:	Cost:
20 extra friends at 50 cents each	$ 9.95
50 extra friends at 40 cents each	$ 19.95
100 extra friends at 30 cents each	$ 29.95
200 friends at 20 cents each	$ 39.95
300 friends at 17 cents each	$ 49.95
500 friends at 14 cents each	$ 69.95
1000 friends at 10 cents each	$ 99.95

Over 1000 friends: $ 99.95 plus .05 per friend over 1000.

VISIT http://ObamasDemons.com TO BUY A LICENSE.